ENDURING

TO THE

END

*Twelve Major Causes of Apostasy and
How to Overcome Them*

ENDURING

TO THE

END

*Twelve Major Causes of Apostasy and
How to Overcome Them*

by

I. Barry Thompson

BONNEVILLE BOOKS
Springville, Utah

ISBN: 1-55517-553-8
v.1

Published by Bonneville Books
An imprint of Cedar Fort, Inc.
925 N. Main Springville, Utah, 84663
www.cedarfort.com

Distributed by:

Typeset by Marny K. Parkin
Cover design by Adam Ford
Cover design © 2001 by Lyle Mortimer

Printed in the United States of America
10 9 8 7 6 5 4 3 2 1
Printed on acid-free paper

 Library of Congress Cataloging-in-Publication Data
> Thompson, Barry, 1929-
> Enduring to the end : twelve major causes of apostasy and how to overcome
> them / by Barry Thompson.
> p. cm.
> Includes bibliographical references.
> ISBN 1-55517-553-8 (pbk. : alk. paper)
> 1. Church of Jesus Christ of Latter-Day Saints--History. 2. Mormon
> Church--History. 3. Apostasy--History. I. Title.
> BX8611 .T48 2001
> 289.3'09--dc21
>   2001003731

To
my wife, Ellen,
and her brother, Daniel A. Keeler,
who gave me insights and encouragement.

FOREWORD

Years ago I was a friend and home teacher to a wonderful bishop. He exhibited many of the virtues and dedication that I desired for myself. He gave priority to his family, a wife and children, while serving well as bishop and as a successful businessman.

Unfortunately, there was one problem that flawed this ideal family. His wife, who came from a pioneer Mormon heritage and who had served as a missionary, had a deep resentment of certain doctrines and practices in the Church. Her criticism persisted in spite of the wonderful attitude and performance of her husband, at least as I saw it.

In due course we both moved to other locations in pursuit of employment. Then after a decade I happened to travel overseas via the distant city where the bishop and his wife were living. Wanting to renew our friendship, I telephoned them to see if we could get together on an overnight layover in their city, and arrangements were made for them to pick me up at the airport upon my arrival.

During the evening, the wife told me how she was now free of all the things that had repressed her over many years. She explained that she no longer believed in God, in priesthood authority, the Church, and the covenants she had previously made. I waited for some response from my good friend, the bishop, whom I had so admired. I sensed that he had long ago decided to live with her rejection of those principles and practices so essential to having the Holy

Spirit, and which had been embraced in sacred covenants, to preserve a marriage and a family for their several children.

Recently I have been told that most of their children are no longer active church members. Furthermore, I was told that the bishop is not active.

In the decades since, I have observed many members who gave long and faithful service to the Church, and have sacrificed to rear their children in the fullness of Latter-day Saint tradition and testimony. Then, when the great demands of family and Church have passed, they have withdrawn from the call of Church service and attendance, some to inactivity and others from membership. It is as if they had done their part, and now they wanted to "enjoy life," free from the demands of schedules and authority.

Because so many of those I have described have been, and are, friends I have loved and admired, their courses have caused me to ponder the many scriptural admonitions regarding the necessity of **enduring to the end** (Moro. 3:3; D&C 14:7; 63:20, 47; 101:5; 121:8, 29).

Enduring may involve many things: paying tithing and offerings, sickness and poor health, debt, contention in the home, and adversity in every aspect of our lives. It would seem that we are constantly being tested, requiring that we be vigilant, and be worthy of the guidance of the Holy Spirit, to **endure to the end.**

What may be a challenge or a trial to one member or person, may not be so for another, in part due to choices that we make, or due to circumstances that come to us unexpectedly and\or uninvited. For example, poor health can come as easily to the rich as to the poor, requiring responses quite diverse: medical treatment, priesthood blessings, prayer and faith, patient waiting for the inevitable, and/or the healing from provident living practices.

In contemplating why some of the early Saints **endured** great trials and persecution, while others chose to apostatize in some form or other, we cannot know what each person brought to that decision. Furthermore, we cannot see what influence other persons had upon them, nor the extent that the adversary played. Each of us is so much an individual, with many experiences from the past weighing upon each new challenge that arises. However, we can observe their cumulative acts, and thoughts expressed, that reveal their, and our, character and values that will determine our responses to conditions that are sought after, or are forced upon us.

Someone suggested to me that he felt that many of the early Saints were called forth to perform a certain task, a calling, a great sacrifice, with heavenly assistance. Evidently they were then "released" from this special role, and heavenly help, to rely on their lesser persona to persevere by more normal means, i.e., prayer, faith, priesthood blessings, advice from friends, or reliance on one's experience, etc.

In trying to ascertain the causes of the faithful endurance, or apostasy, two major sources were the Lord's declarations in the Doctrine and Covenants and statements by the Prophet Joseph Smith and his successors. Of the latter, it should be recognized that these men were subject to personal bias. Another source, disciplinary councils, not infrequently brought forth claims against various brethren regarding their faithful exercise of duty and personal behavior; however these proceedings and decisions may have been driven by personal rivalries and animosity.

Of particular interest to me is the **failure to endure** by these men and women, after they had experienced glorious spiritual manifestations and/or enjoyed the companionship of the Prophet Joseph Smith and other valiant Saints. Some saw the Savior, angels, and their departed ancestors, while many lived in the home of Joseph or sat in councils with him and the apostles; and most of them witnessed, participated in, or received, miraculous healings, not once but on many occasions.

The willingness of the brethren and their families to

accept mission calls or to perform other difficult tasks was often overwhelming, in view of their meager resources to sustain both the missionary, and also his wife and children, while he was gone from home. Because the Saints were kept on the move due to persecution in New York, Kirtland, Missouri and Nauvoo, few of the families had comfortable shelter, and rarely any reserves to hold over the family with the breadwinner gone, sometimes for several years. Over and above these temporal conditions, there was the mental and spiritual burden placed upon the mother to rear her children and provide for their temporal needs.

The difference between **enduring** and **apostasy** often appears to be the willingness, the humility, to accept chastisement from the Lord or from the Prophet, and to then correct the problem, although not always quickly. Those whose pride, and/or motives that were not right, caused them to bridle at such counsel, often started them further along the road to inactivity and rebellion. All too often, the behavior that brought forth the rebuke or counsel was over trivial things. An example is the calling of Symonds Ryder, who was offended over the incorrect spelling of his name as "Rider" in his written call to serve as a missionary. He reasoned that a prophet that could not spell correctly his name, probably could not be trusted to declare the will of the Lord.

Men and women of all persuasions were attracted to this new religion, with its new and positive doctrine and the gifts of the Spirit that were manifested in marvelous ways. Some were wrought upon profoundly by the Holy Spirit, while others were fascinated by the dynamics of its growth and the charisma of its leaders. Most of them were soon given opportunities to take their enthusiasm for the gospel to their families and friends, or to strangers in near and distant places. If they sought for, and were blessed by, the Holy Spirit, they were strengthened in both body and spirit, which prepared them for the trials that would surely come. But to engage in these early challenges without seeking, or receiving the Spirit, they were often disappointed and left in a condition vulnerable to doubts given them by the adversary, or even from well-meaning friends.

Pondering the need for **enduring to the end**, it occurred to me that the early Saints in this last dispensation **endured** much, which caused some of them to rise to heroic performance, and others to apostasy, infamy and misery. A great many received glorious manifestations of the Spirit, saw the Savior or angels, performed or witnessed miracles, labored with and were taught by Joseph Smith, Brigham Young and other spiritual giants of both sexes. Witnessing physically, and in the Spirit, marvellous events of the Restoration, they were able to **endure** tests that amaze us who live in conditions so comfortable compared to the early Saints. We may ask ourselves, "Could we have **endured** as they did?" Some of us could, and some of us could, or would, not.

Almost all of the Church members profiled in the companion volume, *Profiles of Enduring and Apostasy*, experienced special callings, marvelous spiritual manifestations, and the witness of the Holy Spirit. These experiences set them on the high road to receive even greater blessings and opportunities for service in the latter-day work of the Restoration of the Fullness of Times. I have long been curious about what happened to these Saints, after their time of glory. After the glory, how did they deal with daily life and new challenges to their testimonies and resolve? Did they wish to "enjoy life" and hold back, or take the easy way, instead of holding to the rod and **enduring** that which they were given to **endure**?

As I examined the lives of some of my own pioneer ancestors, both men and women, and then others more famous or infamous, I determined that I could learn from them many things that would help me to **endure** as they did. As I researched more of the lives of these early Saints, I became convinced that they were much like us, but in a much different circumstance.

Consequently, I chose ninety-nine men, six women, and eleven non-members, who were involved in the establishment of the Church in New York, Ohio, Missouri and Illinois and Utah. A majority of them were pioneers, although many did not survive to cross the plains to Utah. Many were converts from Europe. Of the 105 members profiled, forty were excommunicated or left the Church, and only eight returned to the Church by baptism.

It is unfortunate that more persons were not profiled, inasmuch as while they may have been less famous, they were equally faithful. While they may not have enjoyed the special experiences or personal relationships of those persons I have profiled, they were strengthened by the teachings of the restored gospel, the Holy Spirit, and the example and counsel of their inspired and dedicated leaders.

In addition to the 116 profiles of men and women, Saints and Gentiles, friends and persecutors, there is a chapter dealing with the wives of intrepid missionaries of the restored gospel, or the Mormon Battalion, who stayed behind with children, elderly, handicapped and the poor. As we consider their circumstances, we are awed by their devotion and perseverance in conditions desperate and pitiful. To me, they are the most heroic of the latter-day servants of God. They performed admirably alone, or with the help of neighbors, and their dutiful children. But some gave up, physically and/or spiritually, after enduring illness, suffering and persecution day after day after day.

Finally then, I endeavored to determine what caused these early Saints to remain faithful to, or to apostatize from, the brotherhood of the Church of Christ and the covenants they had made. In this examination I have sought the opinions of several Church members whom I admire and who have some insight into the events and people of the early days of the Church. Their views are greatly appreciated and have contributed much to my evaluation of the causes of faithfulness and apostasy.

My hope is that what those early Saints **endured** may give us pause and a warning of the dangers along the path to the glorious tree that Lehi and Nephi saw in vision. Do we face similar perils and temptations? Are we equal to our forefathers, although our challenges are much different? What can we learn from their lives that will prepare us **to endure to the end**?

After the glory of our personal experiences, are we prepared to stay the course?

Elder Sterling W. Still recalled the epic story of the Odyssey wherein Ulysses led his valiant Greek warriors on a 10-year journey to their homes in Ithaca. They had fought and won a long and brutal conflict called the "Trojan War." They were anxious to return to their families. Little did they know the greater perils they must conquer as they sailed home.

The story tells of man-eating giants, bewitching sirens, terrible monsters, frightening ghosts, roaring whirlwinds, hair-raising adventures and romantic interludes. The blind author, Homer, reveals the strengths and weaknesses of these famous heroes for our examination.

They would encounter the Lotus-Eaters, where eating the magic fruit made them forget about their families and their responsibilities, preferring to live in dreamy forget-fulness and indolent enjoyment.

On the island of Circe, the enchantress held them and changed some of them into swine. Passing the island where lived the bewitching sirens, Ulysses forced them to put wax in their ears so that they would not become enslaved by the sirens. Despite all of Ulysses' counsel and attention to bring his heroes home, he alone arrived at last in Ithaca.

In his absence of 20 years Ulysses learned that there were as many problems at home as he had survived while away.

Frequently, like Ulysses and his men, we win the great wars of our lives and then lose our way, while doing some comparatively easy, simple thing. All of the warriors survived the ten-year war, only to succumb to the enchantments of the easy trip home. Like the Greeks, the things that try us the most are not the hard, tough battles or the difficult problems, it is the lethargy, the indecision, the sloth, the little evils, the bad habits, and the wrong attitudes. We must win the great battles of life, and also retain the will and strength to finish the task, to **endure to the end.**

Plutarch reminds: **"It is not in the lists that the victors are made, but after the contests are over."**

NOTE: Whenever the scriptures and comments from other sources are cited, they are exact quotations, including misspelled words or improper grammar. In the quotations from the *Journal of Discourses,* the year they were given, in brackets [ ], follows the name of the speaker, indicating to the reader the time lapsed between the events mentioned and the date of reference by the speaker.

CAUSES OF APOSTASY

In the tumultuous years of the early Church up to the exodus from Nauvoo in 1846, there were several crucial events that precipitated crisis and apostasy among the members of the rapidly growing Church.

Membership in a new church that claimed to have the fullness of the gospel, and to be the only true church, brought with it great expectations of performance and devotion, plus the unwelcome persecution from established religions, which was more than many new converts were prepared for.

The failure in 1837 of the Kirtland Safety Society Anti-Banking Company, a quasi-bank, caused many to seriously question the judgment and/or inspiration of the Prophet Joseph.

This loss of faith in the Prophet spilled over to Missouri. Compounded by the intense persecution and the imprisonment of Joseph Smith and many of his close associates in late 1838, great fear arose among many of the Saints in Missouri.

In Nauvoo the practice of plural marriage, coupled with their gentile neighbors' concerns over Mormon political power, culminated in the martyrdom of Joseph and Hyrum Smith in 1844.

The exodus from Nauvoo in early 1846 into the western wilderness was the final straw for many Saints, especially those who relied so greatly on the charisma and authority of Joseph Smith.

Of the 105 Mormons profiled in the companion volume *Profiles of Apostasy and Enduring,* forty were excommunicated or left the Church, and only eight returned to church membership. On the other hand, several of these ex-members expressed later a desire to return to brotherhood with the Saints and the companionship of the Spirit that they had enjoyed before their words and acts of rebellion.

Based on chastisement cited by the Lord in the Doctrine and Covenants and from comments of the latter-day prophets of the Church, the most frequent and serious causes that lead to apostasy are **criticism of Church leaders, unrepented sins, neglect of duty, ignoring personal revelation/inspiration, prosperity and riches.**

Upon close examination, **pride** and **worldly desires** underlie most of the aforementioned causes, as well as many others: **ambition, not seeking the spirit, fear of persecution, intellectual superiority, trifling affairs, polygamy,** etc.

In April Conference 1989, President Ezra Taft Benson warned the Saints to "beware of **pride,** lest ye become as the Nephites of old (D&C 38:39) . . . (it existed) in the pre-mortal council . . . the central feature of **pride** is enmity toward God and enmity toward our fellow men."

Since men do not have direct access to Deity, their enmity is directed toward His work and servants.

No doubt many of those men felt they had qualifications superior to Joseph Smith's. Many of them were older, better educated, experienced in gospel scholarship and in various professions. Moreover, they had enjoyed special spiritual manifestations and blessings.

At the same time, Joseph was human and made mistakes, which his accusers and critics magnified in the wisdom of hindsight. His kindness and willingness to forgive others were viewed by some as weaknesses unbecoming a prophet of God. Had they recalled the shortcomings and mistakes of Biblical prophets (e.g., Moses, Elisha, Elijah, Jonah, Peter), they could have realized that God's servants are not inspired in all events of life, and that sometimes wisdom came to them from mistakes and poor judgment.

Joseph's two most prominent companions, Oliver Cowdery and Sidney Rigdon, felt and expressed their superiority to Joseph. Both were older and better educated. Both had been designated Spokesman for Joseph, as was Aaron for Moses. Both were proven and successful missionaries. Both had claims of equal authority, particularly Oliver as the Second Elder and Assistant President, and Sidney as a Counselor in the First Presidency who was sustained as a Prophet, Seer and Revelator in 1841.

Other men, with lesser claims to authority or personal wisdom, believed that their achievement and reputation merited special consideration, or it excused them from the disciplines of the Church and their particular duties or positions of responsibility.

Invariably, the road to apostasy is linked to the loss (of the influence) of the **Holy Spirit.** When unrighteous thoughts lead to words and actions against God's chosen and His kingdom, always involving a loss of humility (*my will, not thine*), then the man or woman is caught in a deadly downward spiral to apostasy. Satan is ever ready to offer justification and encouragement to the offended or ambitious person.

Joseph possessed and understood the power and requirements of the **Holy Spirit.** He knew that humility and repentance were prerequisites to having the **spirit.** His understanding came early from various experiences in his ministry.

From the awesome experience with the Father and the Son in the Sacred Grove, and later appearances of the great prophets—Adam, Moses, Elijah, Noah, Moroni—Joseph recognized his own modest talents and achievements, and his need to be both humble and repentant.

In the weeks following his acquisition of the gold plates, he was constantly prompted by the **Spirit** in keeping the plates safe from thieves and persecutors, who undoubtedly were aided by the adversary.

He experienced the great power of the **spirit** to translate the initial 116 manuscript pages. To succumb to the entreaties of Martin Harris to show the manuscript to his family, despite the Lord's repeated refusal, and the resulting agony and despair at the loss of the manuscript, as well as the **spirit,** he was brought to the depths of repentance. Only after weeks of entreating the Lord to forgive him was he able to regain the plates and the **spirit** and be allowed to resume translating.

Emma, as his scribe, reported in awe how Joseph, after a lunch break or other interruption, would return to translating the gold plates at the exact word where he left off an hour earlier. Oliver Cowdery likewise marveled that Joseph could repeat a phrase or sentence exactly as earlier translated from the plates, or in dictating a revelation.

All of these manifestations of the **spirit** were understood and appreciated by the young prophet Joseph. By them he was well aware of the need for humility and repentance so that he would be a fit vessel to receive the **Holy Spirit** and to know for certain what he was to do.

In the following chapters we will consider the behavior (lives) of these early Saints as they dealt with their glorious experiences and ordeals—some adversely, and others who grew in faith and testimony.

After the glory of their experiences, how did they endure in their ongoing trials, adversities and daily life?

CRITICISM OF CHURCH LEADERS

One of the greatest causes of apostasy in the early days of the Restored Church, as well as in our time, is personal criticism of Church leaders. In the earlier days, grievances were directed toward Joseph Smith, whereas in our day it is the Bishops who bear most of the wrath of unhappy members. As these disgruntled members regress to rebellion and eventual excommunication, however, their anger is often directed toward the General Authorities and the Church in general.

When the Church was expanding from a few families in New York state, and then gaining many new converts in Kirtland, almost everyone knew the Prophet Joseph. Most of these early members were involved in remarkable spiritual manifestations—healings, heavenly visions, speaking and interpreting in tongues, or powerful impressions of the Spirit. Their conversion and baptism were often founded on such external signs, a fragile foundation from which to withstand the storms of persecution that Satan would mount against them personally, and against the young Prophet.

Joseph Smith was only 24 when the Church was organized on April 6, 1830. He occasionally made some mistakes as he assumed the immense task of translating the gold plates, receiving the Holy Priesthood, organizing the Church of Jesus Christ, and accomplishing these and other tasks with a variety of people who were older and steeped in traditions and agenda contrary to the new order. No doubt these converts who participated with Joseph in bringing forth the "restoration of all things" had high expectations of the Prophet; after all, it was the **true** church, the **fullness** of the Gospel, the **holy priesthood of God,** and the marvelous manifestations of the **Holy Ghost** with all the **gifts of the Spirit.**

Any words or acts by Joseph that did not measure up to their high expectations would be subject to question, then doubt, then protest, then rebellion and finally hostility.

President Spencer W. Kimball speaks well to this condition:

> Apostasy usually begins with question and doubt and criticism. The seeds of doubt are planted by unscrupulous or misguided people, and seldom directed against the doctrine at first, but more often against the **leaders**. . . . They who garnish the sepulchers of the dead prophets begin now by stoning the living ones. They return to the pronouncements of the dead **leaders** and interpret them to be incompatible with present programs. . . . They say that while the gospel and the Church are divine, the **leaders** are fallen . . . becomes an active resistance, and frequently the blooming apostate begins to air his views and to crusade. . . . He generally wants all the blessings of the Church, membership, its priesthood, its temple privileges, and expects them from the **leaders** of the Church, though at the same time claiming that those same **leaders** have departed from the path. He now expects persecution and adopts a martyr complex, and when finally excommunication comes he associates himself with other apostates (Edward L. Kimball, *Teachings of Spencer W. Kimball,* 462).

It is perplexing how some Kirtland apostates such as Ezra Booth and Symonds Ryder, who were members for such a short time, and likely had marginal testimonies, would have become so violent and vindictive toward Joseph Smith. Booth published several letters in a local newspaper filled with lies regarding the Prophet and the

Church. Ryder, defecting over the misspelling of his name (Rider) in his mission certificate, was one of the ringleaders of the mob that tarred and feathered Joseph and Sidney Rigdon at the Johnson farm in Hiram, Ohio. One can suppose that the adversary gained great control over them to cause such bitter actions.

Recalling such trying times, Orson Pratt observed:

> It seems as though the adversary, in the day in which we live, seeks, by every means in his power, to undermine the influence and the authority of the man whom God has called to preside over His people. . . . In the days of Joseph, he was the man against whom all the enemies of truth hurled their malicious shots; his life was sought, his character assailed, and his influence was scoffed at, despised and killed (Orson Pratt, *Journal of Discourses*, 13:70). [1883]

The case of the Kirtland Safety Society was much more complicated in its conception, operation and the consequences of its failure on the testimonies and reactions of many members who were involved. In 1836 the Church was growing rapidly and many Saints were pouring into the area in need of employment, housing and credit. Some of the leading brethren conceived that a Kirtland Safety Society Bank could be organized to make capital out of idle land. It would be backed by Mormon land and the sale of stock to members. With land as the capital base, the bank could issue notes in the form of loans to individuals and purchasers and secure them with mortgages on the land. The mortgages would then be used as assets to issue more notes. Notes could also be issued on deposits received.

Unfortunately, the Ohio Legislature refused to grant a banking license. The founders then decided to form a joint stock company with note-issuing powers. This "bank" was called the Kirtland Safety Society Antibanking Company. When the "bank" was started in January 1837, the spirit of speculation was prevalent throughout the nation. Many of the members who had been faithful were caught up in the prospect of becoming rich.

> The directors of that bank were members of the Church, and they were determined to sustain the credit of that money. Warren Parrish was the teller of the bank, and a number of other men who (later) apostatized were officers. They took out of the vault, unknown to the President or Cashier, a hundred thousand dollars, and sent their agents around among the brethren to purchase their farms, wagons, cattle, horses and everything they could get hold of. The brethren would gather up this money and put it into the bank, and those traitors would steal it and send it out to buy again, and they continued to do so until the plot was discovered and payment stopped. It was the cursed apostates—their stealing and robberies, and their infernal villainies that prevented that bank being conducted as the Prophet designed. If they had followed the counsel of Joseph, there is not a doubt but that it would have been the leading bank in Ohio, probably of the nation. It was founded upon safe principles, and would have been a safe and lasting institution.(George A. Smith, *Journal of Discourses*, 11:11). [1864]

Joseph Smith was wont to comment, "As the fruits of this spirit, evil surmisings, fault-finding, dissension, disunion and apostasy followed in quick succession, and it seemed as though all the powers of earth and hell were combining their influence in an especial manner to overthrow the Church at once, and make a final end" (Joseph Smith, *History of the Church*, vol. 2:487).

In May 1837 the bubble burst, land values plummeted, and the bank failed. Before Joseph returned from a mission to Michigan, a group including members of the Twelve and other priesthood leaders had mounted a campaign to depose Joseph as Prophet, which was barely averted by a stout defense by Brigham Young to the effect that God had appointed Joseph as Prophet, so there was nothing the apostates could do about it, which was seconded by John Taylor, who had come down from Canada.

In the midst of this crisis, Joseph was told by the Spirit to send Heber C. Kimball to open a mission to England with six companions. To lose these faithful supporters at such a critical time was evidence that Joseph was obedient to the Lord through the Spirit.

In September 1837 several of the apostates were disfellowshipped and soon after fifty were excommunicated by the Kirtland High Council, including the Johnson family, John and his two apostle sons, Luke and Lyman. This only fanned the rage of the apostates, so that Joseph and Sidney had to flee in late December 1837 for Missouri, to be followed in the ensuing months by the remainder of the faithful in Kirtland.

This dissension did not stay in Kirtland, as several of those who came to Far West brought with them doubts about the Prophet Joseph and the bank failure. They suggested that if Joseph was truly the Prophet, why did he not prevent its formation in the first place, or at least intervene when the bank officers began violating the mission of the bank.

The Presidency of the Church in Missouri (in effect a stake presidency), composed of David and John Whitmer and W. W. Phelps, felt they were equal to the First Presidency in Kirtland, and therefore, independent in all matters. They had been infected by the doubts of the Kirtland conspiracy. In March 1838, the High Council in Far West excommunicated the Missouri Presidency for land dealings and not keeping the Word of Wisdom. Then all of the surviving members of the Whitmer family were either excommunicated or left the Church, including son-in-law, Oliver Cowdery.

Joseph F. Smith observed that a member's antipathy

toward a Church **leader** is not cause for apostasy:

> notwithstanding my dislike for certain men, I know
> that the Gospel is true, and that God is with his peo-
> ple, and that if I will do my duty and keep His com-
> mandments, the clouds will roll by and mists will
> disappear, the spirit of the Lord will come more fully
> to my relief, and by and by every wrong thing will yet
> be made right. . . . If a man were to sit in judgment on
> his Bishop . . . he would be like some others I have
> heard of, John and David Whitmer, and William
> McLellin, and William Smith, and many others . . .
> firmly convinced that they never apostatized and
> became wicked, and (they) are the only members of
> the Church in good standing (Joseph F. Smith, *Journal
> of Discourses*, 24:190-91). [1883]

The intense persecution that began in Jackson County
and followed the Saints to Clay, Ray, and Caldwell counties
caused considerable fear and frustration among the Saints.
Two fiery speeches by Sidney Rigdon, one called the "salt
sermon" on June 17, 1838, that served as a warning that
Mormon dissenters would be "cast out and trodden under
foot of men." And the other on July 4, warned apostates
and persecutors alike that the Mormons would not tolerate
further abuse and pillaging. While many of the dissenters
chose to leave the area, the old settlers resented Rigdon's
promise of counteraction.

To oppose the mob activities that followed the fight
with Missouri ruffians at Gallatin on election day in
August, a military group was formed by the Saints which
came to be called the Danites. An ambitious convert named
Sampson Avard took control of the Danites and caused
them to actively raid and punish some of the old settlers.
Finally a battle between a large Missouri mob and Mormon
defenders occurred at Crooked River that ignited mob and
military action, including the **Exterminating Order** by

Governor Lilburn Boggs.

Following the massacre of the defenseless Saints at Haun's Mill and the arrest and trial of Joseph Smith and many of the Church **leaders,** many fearful Saints left and were never seen again among the faithful. Avard was the chief witness against the brethren at the mock trial at Far West.

Heber C. Kimball commented that, "Now there are a great many people have broken off from this Church . . . but have they not withered? Yea, and so will you if you turn away from it, and if you refuse to obey the counsel that is given you, you will wither away. . . . We are the people of God, and we cannot prosper upon any other principle than to cleave to this work" (Heber C. Kimball, *Journal of Discourses*, 1:207). [1852]

As the faithful struggled across wintry wastes of upper Missouri in 1839 to cross the Mississippi River to safety in Illinois, many others decided to disavow their membership in the Church to stay on their farms in Missouri, while still others dispersed to the east. Wilford Woodruff declared in 1880 that, "There is hardly a tithe of the people who have been baptized in water for the remission of sins that have died in the faith. In the United States there are tens of thousands of apostate Mormons" (Wilford Woodruff, *Journal of Discourses*, 21:281–82). [1880]

A period of calm and hope prevailed among the Saints when Joseph led them to settle and develop Nauvoo, Illinois. New converts from England and the Eastern States arrived almost daily in the beautiful city of Nauvoo. But their neighbors worried about the political power of such a large and "solid-voting" block. Lies and warrants for the arrest of Joseph and others only fed this unrest.

During this time of prosperity for the Saints in Nauvoo, a terrific test was given the faithful—polygamy. Even the most faithful were severely tried by this new doctrine, not the least of whom were Joseph's two closest friends, wife

11

Emma and brother Hyrum, both of whom emphatically objected to the principle and practice of it. Other leaders were ready to subvert it to their lustful and base desires. These included two counselors in the First Presidency, John C. Bennett and William Law, and Joseph's brother, William Smith. As many were disciplined for objecting to and/or the malpractice of plural marriage, there arose a vocal and angry clique who hated the Prophet and the Church. They aligned themselves with the growing mob in adjacent localities to call for the blood of Joseph, and the destruction of the Church and the beautiful city of Nauvoo.

Three men who lived through these perilous days give us their observations regarding the faithful and the apostates:

> There were others during Joseph's day, who professed to have the authority he possessed, or, as they said, which he had once possessed. . . . There was a number of elders, among whom were some of the Twelve apostles and one or two of the First Presidency, who banded together and declared that Joseph was a fallen prophet, that he had taught correct doctrines, that he had been an instrument in the hands of God . . . but that he had fallen . . . the wicked hailed them as brethren, consorted with them, became very brotherly, very fraternal, and looked upon them very good, clever fellows . . . Sidney Rigdon . . . James Strang. . . . Others stood up in like manner: John E. Page, Lyman Wight, William Smith and Charles Thompson (George Q. Cannon, *Journal of Discourses*, 13:45–46). [1869]

> I give you a key which brother Joseph Smith used to give in Nauvoo. He said, that the very step of apostasy commenced with losing confidence in the **leaders** of this Church and kingdom, and that whenever you discerned that spirit, you might know that it would lead the possessor of it on the road to apostasy . . . if husbands and wives are quarreling one with another,

I say, there is the spirit of apostasy, there is a place where the Spirit of God does not abide in its fullness (Heber C. Kimball, *Journal of Discourses*, 3:271). [1856]

"Whenever the voice of the people of God, and the authorities in the Church . . . lift up their hands against a man to cut him off from the Church, to withdraw from him the authority of the Priesthood that he has exercised, in every instance without a single exception, from the beginning of this Church until today, God has most signally and wonderfully manifested His approval of their acts and has withdrawn from that man (no matter how great and mighty he may have been in the Church) His power and His blessing. It was so with Oliver Cowdery . . . other men also, six of the original twelve fell into transgression. They were men of ability and talent. . . . Lyman Johnson had wonderful manifestations given to him, Sidney Rigdon, that mighty man, that eloquent man, that spokesman for the Prophet Joseph . . . lifted their hands against him (Joseph) (George Q. Cannon, *Journal of Discourses*, 26:248). [1884]

The Prophet Joseph is purported to have said that "if you will throw a cloak over my faults, I will over yours." Therein lies the secret of surviving the dangerous practice of criticizing our Church **leaders.**

President Gordon B. Hinckley has truly observed:

I knew the Presidents of the Church . . . as well as other General Authorities. I came to know early that they were men, imperfect in some small ways. But I wish to say that I felt they were the best men to be found in this world. They too had to deal with the writings and talks of malcontents and apostates. But the names of their critics have gone down to oblivion. (Gordon B. Hinckley, *Teachings of Gordon B. Hinckley*, 125–26).

While the Bishops and Stake Presidents of the Church

are "learning on the job," they are blessed with the mantle of inspiration, which is the Holy Spirit, to guide them in dealing with the multitude of needs of their flocks. Oftentimes members demand that Bishops solve their problems that have arisen from poor preparation, faulty decisions, violation of covenants, worldly pursuits, and a myriad of other actions or attitudes that require a payment of some kind. When the Bishop does not solve these demands to the satisfaction of his members, doubt or disappointment may start a cycle that leads to criticism, loss of the Spirit, and "kicking against the pricks," until they do not enjoy the association with the Saints.

Since each person is responsible for his own actions and thoughts, he or she must not expect a Church leader to take that responsibility from them. But oftentimes in the magnitude of despair or guilt that can arise when one is facing insistent creditors, abusive spouses, the pain of unrepented sin, and other overwhelming crises, persons may reach out to their Bishop for relief. Not infrequently, the Bishop may respond in some form of chastisement, gently or forcefully, which might not be well received by the seeker. But whatever his counsel, the burden of changing one's life remains with the member.

So what can, or should, one do to steer clear of criticism of Bishops and other Church **leaders**?

One obvious way is to listen to, and keep, the Holy Spirit. When we seek the guidance of the Holy Spirit in dealing with any concern or need, we will be prompted aright. It is the Spirit who will respond to our humble prayer to God for help with any problem we may have with a Church **leader** or member, or with someone in our family. The Lord has counseled his disciples to add fasting to prayer in certain situations.

The Lord has given us ongoing counsel that is found in the scriptures. One scripture that is especially helpful is found in the 121st Section of the Doctrine and Covenants:

> Behold, there are many called, but few are chosen. And why are they not chosen?
>
> Because their hearts are set so much upon the things of this world, and aspire to the honors of men, that they do not learn this one lesson—
>
> That the rights of the priesthood are inseparably connected with the powers of heaven, and that the powers of heaven cannot be controlled nor handled only upon the principles of righteousness.
>
> That they may be conferred upon us, it is true; but when we undertake to cover our sins, or to gratify our pride, our vain ambition, or to exercise control or dominion or compulsion upon the souls of the children of men, in any degree of unrighteousness, behold, the heavens withdraw themselves; the spirit of the Lord is grieved; and when it is withdrawn, Amen to the priesthood or the authority of that man.
>
> Behold, ere he is aware, he is left unto himself, to kick against the pricks, to persecute the saints, and to fight against God.
>
> We have learned by sad experience that it is the nature and disposition of almost all men, as soon as they get a little authority, as they suppose, they will immediately begin to exercise unrighteous dominion.
>
> Hence many are called, but few are chosen.
>
> No power or influence can or ought to be maintained by virtue of the priesthood, only by persuasion, by long-suffering, by gentleness and meekness, and by love unfeigned;
>
> By kindness, and pure knowledge, which shall greatly enlarge the soul without hypocrisy, and without guile—
>
> Reproving betimes with sharpness, when moved upon by the Holy Ghost; and then showing forth afterwards an increase of love toward him whom thou hast reproved, lest he esteem thee to be his enemy;
>
> Let thy bowels also be full of charity towards all

15

men, and to the household of faith, and let virtue garnish thy thoughts unceasingly; then shall thy confidence wax strong in the presence of God; and the doctrine of the priesthood shall distil upon thy soul as the dews from heaven.

The Holy Ghost shall be thy constant companion, and thy scepter an unchanging scepter of righteousness and truth; and thy dominion shall be an everlasting dominion, and without compulsory means it shall flow unto thee forever and ever (D&C 121:34–46).

Sermons and writings of the General Authorities contain much counsel regarding proper respect for Church leaders. *The Miracle of Forgiveness* by President Spencer W. Kimball is an outstanding guide to keeping ourselves worthy of the Lord's blessings, which includes harmony with our **leaders.**

Finally, and probably most difficult for most of us, is the direct approach to negative feelings toward our Church **leaders.** Go to him or her, and discuss in humility your concerns or grievance. Quite likely, you may learn some things that will change your opinions or feelings. Assuming his response will be kindly and sympathetic, the mutual bond between you will be strengthened.

If you are unable to muster the courage of a direct contact, an alternative would be to speak to his file **leader,** i.e., to the Stake President, if you are at odds with your Bishop. The Stake President can give you guidance and/or prepare an interview with your Bishop that will help resolve your concerns.

UNREPENTED SIN

Repentance is one of the least understood principles of the restored gospel. While members of the Church may recite the five to seven "Rs" of repentance, the essential understanding that it includes **Godly sorrow** for one's conscious **violations** of commandments and covenants, and a firm **avowal not to repeat** them, is not well comprehended by many members, active or otherwise.

Usually the sinner has a pang of conscience and feels sorry. However, his or her sorrow may be only for having been caught in the **sin,** or that they are unable to ignore having committed it.

A Bishop of a singles ward recounted an experience with a young sister in his congregation. She insisted on talking to him in the hallway at Church, because she was leaving for out of town prior to the conclusion of the block meetings. Ducking into a vacant classroom, she confessed to the Bishop that she had fornicated during the previous week, but that she was sorry and wanted to confess to her priesthood leader. She assumed that her confession to her Bishop was all that was necessary for her repentance. When the Bishop endeavored to explained that there was much more involved for her obtaining forgiveness, she responded that this was how she had handled it (repentance for a similar act) in the past.

Deliberate **violation** of a law or commandment, assuming that the sinner understood what he or she was doing, obviously demands a greater penalty or chastisement.

Such **sins** of commission are not easily repented of, nor may the sinner be favorably disposed to chastisement. Consequently men like John C. Bennett and Warren Parrish reacted violently to trials before Church councils or rebukes from the Prophet.

Bennett was an ambitious man who determined that he could gain fame and fortune in this progressive and devoted army who surrounded Joseph Smith in Nauvoo. He reasoned that his talents and assistance to Joseph and the Church entitled him to some worldly indulgences on the side, which he could smooth over with a few lies and the exercise of his authority as a Counselor to the First Presidency. Rebukes from Joseph and others were not well received, and the result was increased belligerence and then open rebellion.

Parrish, on the other hand, had served favorably in several callings, including as secretary to the Prophet Joseph. Greed overcame reason in his stealing substantial funds as teller of the Kirtland Safety Society Antibanking Company. Whatever his motive was at the outset, his stealing and concealing it from the bank's management drew him deeper into his perfidy. Although Parrish and his cohorts were the guilty ones, they tried to make Joseph the scapegoat, as he was one of the founders and the inspiration for the whole bank undertaking. Open rebellion ensued, with many of the church leaders joining in an attempt to depose Joseph so that they could take control of the church.

Apostle George A. Smith recalled the consequences of the banking conspiracy as follows:

> I also remember, in the great apostasy which took place in Kirtland, that those who apostatized considered that all the talent of the Church had left it, and yet the work rolled right along, and, so far as they were concerned, they were never missed, and were soon forgotten, and nobody could tell where they

went to. I have occasionally met them twenty or thirty years afterwards, and could hardly tell where they dropped out . . . the work of the Lord does not depend upon us. If we go into darkness, if we let our hearts be filled with covetousness or corruption, or give way to licentiousness, drunkenness, Sabbath-breaking, unbelief, or any crime that corrodes our system or organization, so that our tabernacles become unfit for the Holy Spirit to dwell in, it will withdraw from us, and the light that is in us becomes darkened, and that darkness is so great that we grope as a blind man and wander hither and thither, and those who suffer themselves to be led by these blind men fall into the ditch with them, but the work rolls right along (George A. Smith, *Journal of Discourses*, 17:196). [1874]

While most church members recognize and steer clear of the "big" **sins**, e.g., murder, adultery and fornication, open rebellion, etc., it is the little ones that start us off into forbidden ground. Not infrequently, when these "little things" are discovered, the sinner is offended by such a fuss. He or she may say that others are doing it, or even worse; and anyway, they are not taking anything from their accuser or fellow employees.

Former counselor in the Presiding Bishopric Robert L. Simpson told of a sister who became literally hypnotized by a deck of playing cards until eventually her obsession caused her to give up an important Relief Society calling and the association with her friends to pursue card playing all of the time. He cited a brother who started taking home pencils and other small items from work, then other things more frequently and of greater value, until he was discovered and fired from his job, losing the respect of his family, and the spirit of his calling in the Church (Robert L. Simpson, *Improvement Era*, June 1969, 89–90).

The classic story of Thomas B. Marsh and his wife involving the milk strippings shows that small deceptions can lead to great consequences. When she was accused of withholding her share of milk, she denied it, probably out of pride. Thomas defended her against her accusers in disciplinary courts before the Bishop and the High Council, and finally before the Prophet Joseph Smith. Each time the evidence and multiple witnesses weighed against Sister Marsh. Both she and her husband, who was then President of the Twelve Apostles, remained unrepentant. In due course they apostatized.

> Few would argue the potential spiritual risk of **major sins** like murder or marital infidelity. But what about the person who uses employer's time to complete personal projects, the person who sneaks into a pornographic movie, the student who cheats at school, the person who criticizes others unfairly, or the parent who thinks family home evening is a good idea—for someone else? (Joseph B. Wirthlin, *Ensign*, November 1992, 36).

Elder Hartman Rector, Jr. suggested that "each of us has certain weaknesses that keep us from being as spiritually in tune as we would like to be. . . . We get them from the Lord; the Lord gives us weaknesses so we will be humble. This makes us teachable."

Elder Rector then reminds us that the adversary will discover our weaknesses and try to exploit them. But we may increase our efforts, aided by the blessing of the Holy Spirit, to overcome our weaknesses, or even to make them our strengths (Hartman Rector Jr., *Improvement Era*, June 1970, 102).

When one is on the path to apostasy, his condition may be aptly described, "but when we undertake to cover our **sins**, or to gratify our pride, our vain ambition, or to exercise control or dominion . . . in any degree of unrighteousness, behold, the heavens withdraw themselves; the Spirit of the Lord is grieved . . . is withdrawn . . . ere he is aware, he is left to kick against the pricks, to persecute the saints, and to fight against God" (D&C 121:36–38).

This scripture so aptly applies to Warren Parrish and apostle John Boynton in Kirtland, and to John C. Bennett, the Law brothers, Robert D. Foster, and apostle William Smith in Nauvoo.

John Boynton was a man of considerable ability, having in 1890 thirty-six patents listed with the U.S. Patent Office. Despite serving three missions and being called as one of the original Twelve Apostles, John was attracted to worldly pursuits. He became involved with the failure of the Kirtland Safety Society bank, and then in the conspiracy to oust Joseph Smith as the Prophet of the Church. Although he "confessed" and was reinstated to the Twelve, he soon after repudiated his confession and returned to his worldly and evil ways.

William McLellin was an early convert and one of the original Twelve Apostles. In D&C 66 the Lord warned him that he should repent, and then in the 90th Section He repeated the warning. At William's trial before a Bishop's Court at Far West in 1838, he admitted to various **sins.** He felt justified because he had no confidence in the leaders of the church, consequently he did not wish to repent. He was cut off for "unbelief and apostasy."

William and Wilson Law and Robert D. Foster engaged in fornication and other sinful activities, while enjoying high callings in the church. Reacting resentfully to chastisement and subsequently at a trial which resulted in their excommunication, these men fought the church and plotted and participated in the martyrdom of Joseph and Hyrum Smith. Years later, Foster lamented his actions and unwillingness to repent, when his earlier **sins** were brought to light and would have been easier to overcome.

The apostasy of William Smith, the younger brother of the Prophet, is puzzling in light of the great faithfulness of the Smith family. His inability to control his terrible temper, and his assumption that he should inherit the authority of his brothers, provoked dissension among the Saints and opposition from the Twelve who were leading the church. In October 1845 the General Conference dropped William from the office of Apostle and Patriarch due to his "general looseness and recklessness of character," in part due to his joining John C. Bennett in lustful activities. He remained **unrepentant** and defiant, although years later he did seek to negotiate a restoration of his apostleship in exchange for joining and bringing his name and legitimacy to the church in Utah.

Another aspect of **sin** and repentance is the "quickie confession." Joseph Smith declared, "Repentance is a thing that cannot be trifled with every day. Daily transgression and daily repentance is not that which is pleasing in the sight of God." This was plainly shown in the case mentioned above with the young woman who was in a hurry to confess.

A Bishop told of an outstanding young man who came in for an interview to serve a mission and to receive the Melchizedek Priesthood. When asked if he was morally clean, he answered in the affirmative. But the Bishop was prompted to ask about specific actions that are covered by that question, and the response was that the future missionary had engaged in this forbidden act in the past. When asked when it last occurred, he admitted that it was the night previous. There was little doubt that he knew it was wrong, and that he was sorry for doing it. But his understanding of repentance was limited—he either hoped that his quick remorse was sufficient, or he did not think his **sin** was so grievous that he needed to undertake the full burden of repentance. His subsequent repentance included an expanded understanding of this great principle from studying *The Miracle of Forgiveness* and an application of his new awareness.

There was a man in Missouri who said he did not believe in Joseph Smith, because he said he was not a true Prophet. Why? Because the revelations say, "If any man committeth adultery, he shall lose the Spirit of God and apostatize. Now, (said he) I have committed adultery, and have not apostatized." You can be the judge where he was. He did not see that he had apostatized, when he discarded Joseph Smith as a false prophet. (John Taylor, *Journal of Discourses*, 7:325). [1859]

President Gordon B. Hinckley observed:

My heart goes out to Peter (after he denied Christ three times). So many of us are so much like him. We pledge our loyalty; we affirm our determination to be of good courage; we declare, sometimes even publicly, that come what may we will do the right thing, that we will stand for the right cause, that we will be true to ourselves and to others.

Then the pressures begin to build. Sometimes these are social pressures. Sometimes they are personal appetites. Sometimes they are false ambitions. There is a softening of discipline. There is capitulation. And then there is remorse, self-accusation, and bitter tears of regret (Gordon B. Hinckley, *Ensign*, May 1979).

Since **unrepentant sin** is a major cause of apostasy, what can we do to eliminate it from our personal lives? The answer is obvious—repent!

A consideration of the famous "Rs" provides some useful guidance: **Recognition, Remorse, Resolution, Restitution and Reformation.**

Recognition comes to one when he or she understands the principle or commandment that has been broken. There are **sins** of omission, wherein we have not known or understood the law we have violated. But for the most part, the sinner is usually sufficiently aware that he has done wrong. Thus, we have the responsibility to discover what the Lord and our fellow men expect of us—those laws and commandments that lead us to righteous living.

23

Remorse is the sorrow and pain that grips our soul for our acts and words that have caused God and others to suffer in body or spirit. Where our errors have merely violated natural laws, we may not have the depth of sorrow that comes from spiritual or moral **transgression.** But those sins that have caused sorrow, injury, corruption, immorality, loss of trust or of reputation, and other offenses of others will exact considerable anguish from us, depending upon the seriousness of the offense and the degree of our soul-searching.

Resolution represents our commitment never to commit that **sin** again. This commitment cannot come in the quick expression of "I'm Sorry!" to either God or to the person(s) we offended. Furthermore, our resolve will require reinforcement, as our memory fades and/or we are distracted by the myriad of events that invade our lives each passing day. A good time for this reinforcement is in our quiet moments that include personal prayers and pondering the scriptures.

Restitution is one of the most difficult tasks in the process of repentance. To face those whom we have offended can be most daunting. This is especially true when we have taken from them something that we cannot restore—chastity, physical injuries, and immoral ideas and acts we may have taught and practiced with them. We must be prepared to receive their negative reaction to our regret and desire to make things right with them. They may not forgive us, or even meet us. They may revile and attack us. Whether we like it or not, this effort to restore that which we took or caused is one of the most cathartic blessings of the process of repentance.

Reformation is identified as the turning from our old ways of **sin** to a new man. We are to be re-formed into one who will not repeat the **sin** from which we are repenting. Like resolution, this effort needs on-going reinforcement.

24

Because we usually live each day with the same friends, same job, same home, same family, we may be facing the conditions that precipitated our previous **sin**. Thus, good counsel often directs us to change many of these influences so that we can make new habits and friends that will reinforce us in our resolve to do right.

Let me emphasize that repentance is so difficult if one cannot, or will not, change the people and circumstances that have contributed to his previous **transgression(s)**. This is amply borne out in the apostasy of the Johnson family in Kirtland, the extended Whitmer family in Missouri, and the Laws/Higbees/Fosters in Nauvoo, who fed on the **sin** and weakness of each other, together with the unholy companionship of the adversary.

President Joseph F. Smith declared that:

> True repentance is not only sorrow for **sins**, and humble penitence and contrition before God, but it involves the necessity of turning away from them [sins], a discontinuance of all evil practices and deeds, a thorough reformation of life, a vital change from evil to good, from vice to virtue, from darkness to light. Not only so, but make restitution, so far as it is possible, for all the wrongs we have done, to pay our debts, and restore to God and man their rights—that which is due to them from us. This is true repentance, and the exercise of the will and all the powers of body and mind is demanded, to complete this glorious work of repentance (Joseph F. Smith, *Gospel Doctrine*, 123).

> To avoid this impure condition [impure thoughts], we must stop the flow into our minds of these unhealthy and unwholesome streams of experiences and thoughts. Evil acts are preceded by unrighteous thoughts, and unrighteous thoughts are born of vulgar stories, jokes, pictures, conversations, and a myriad of other evils or foolish products.

> Vulgarity may be considered in a couple of ways: first, as an expression of personal weakness;

second, as a contribution to a personal weakness. Some demonstrate or express a personal weakness when they tell jokes or stories about the body and its functions, suggestive comments about women or girls, speak crudely of bodily parts or sexual matters. Some contribute to this personal weakness when they read filthy magazines, watch unwholesome movies, television shows and videos, or remain in a group where unclean discussions occur (Bishop H. Burke Petersen, *Ensign*, September 1984, 32).

There is a major difference this time [compared to Noah's time]: God has saved for the final inning some of his stronger and most valiant children, who will help bear off the kingdom triumphantly. . . . You are the generation that must be prepared to meet your God. . . . The final outcome is certain—the forces of righteousness will finally win. But what remains to be seen is where each of us personally, now and in the future, will stand in this battle. . . . (Ezra Taft Benson at BYU, *Ensign*, April 1987, 73).

President Spencer W. Kimball warned us: "**Repent or Perish.**" His warning then reminded us of the words of Jesus and Abinadi:

For behold, I, God, have suffered these things for all, that they might not suffer if they would repent; But if they would not repent they must suffer even as I. Which suffering caused myself, even God, the greatest of all, to tremble because of pain, and to bleed at every pore, and to suffer both body and spirit. . . . (D&C 19:16–18).

But remember that he that persists in his own carnal nature, and goes on in the ways of **sin** and rebellion against God, remaineth in his fallen state and the devil hath all power over him. Therefore, he is as though there was no redemption made, being an enemy to God; and also is the devil an enemy to God (Mosiah 16:5).

Alma the Younger, who understood both **sin** and **repentance** so well, exclaimed:

> O that I were an angel, and could have the wish of mine heart, that I might go forth and speak with the trump of God, with a voice to shake the earth, and cry **repentance** unto every people!
>
> Yea, I would declare unto every soul, as with the voice of thunder, **repentance** and the plan of redemption, that they should **repent** and come unto our God, that there might not be more sorrow upon the face of the earth (Alma 29:1–2).

NEGLECT OF DUTY

In each of the dispensations of the gospel the Lord has given his chosen people direction about their **duty**. Not long after Adam and Eve had been driven from the Garden of Eden, an angel appeared and asked him, "Why dost thou offer sacrifices unto the Lord? And Adam said unto him: I know not, save the Lord commanded me." (Pearl of Great Price, Moses 5:6)

Many **duties** are simple, while others may require study, contemplation and the help of the Holy Spirit to meet the standards set by God, or man.

Our **duty** is a necessary part of the Lord's injunction to us to become perfect as He and the Father are. These directions to us are among the most powerful and relevant in the scriptures.

Old Testament

To the children of Israel who had departed servitude in Egypt and were en route to freedom in the promised land, He gave the Ten Commandments: the first four commandments concern man's **duty to God,** and the last six refer to man's **duty to man,** with the *fifth* specifically referring to one's parents.

Book of Mormon

To Nephi and his family the Lord gave some difficult tasks as they were leaving their comfortable home in Jerusalem to go forth into the unknown. Nephi testified in faith: "I will go and do the things which the Lord hath commanded, for I know that the Lord giveth no commandments unto the children of men, save he shall prepare a way for them that they may accomplish the thing which he commandeth them." (1 Nephi 3:7) What a marvelous assurance this declaration must have been to Joseph Smith as he translated the gold plates, having already experienced considerable danger and persecution up to that time.

Doctrine and Covenants

The month following the calling and ordaining of the Twelve Apostles in Kirtland, they met in council, confessing their individual weaknesses and shortcomings, expressing repentance and seeking the further guidance of the Lord. On that date, March 28, 1835, Joseph Smith received a mighty revelation on the priesthood, at the conclusion of which the Lord proclaimed:

> Wherefore, now let every man learn his **duty**, and to act in the office in which he is appointed, in all diligence. He that is slothful shall not be counted worthy to stand, and he that learns not his **duty** and shows himself not approved shall not be counted worthy to stand (D&C 107:99–100).

George Q. Cannon, then a Counselor to President Wilford Woodruff, gave the following counsel:

> He [God] is ready to bless every man in His Church who will magnify his office and calling. He is ready to bestow the gifts and qualifications of that office upon every man according to his diligence and faithfulness before Him. But the idle man, the slothful man, the man that shirks his responsibility, the man who avoids **duty** . . . every man that does this, God will take from him His gifts and His blessings; He will withdraw them and give them to the faithful one. He

will clothe His faithful servants with the power that belongs to the Priesthood in proportion to the diligence and faithfulness in seeking to magnify their calling and to live near unto their God (George Q. Cannon, *Journal of Discourses*, 26:62). [1884]

Many of those who encountered the Prophet Joseph, even prior to the organization of the Church, were converted, and received testimonies of the restored gospel. It was not uncommon for them to approach the Prophet and ask him to inquire of the Lord as to their responsibilities and **duties.** John, David and Peter Whitmer Jr. asked the Prophet if he would inquire of the Lord as to what they might do—what was their **duty** as men who had recently received the testimony of the truth. When the Prophet made inquiry, each of them were given similar instructions (D&C 14, 14–16): "Behold, blessed are you for this thing. . . . And now, behold, I say unto you, that the thing which will be of most worth unto you will be to declare repentance unto this people, that you may bring souls unto me, that you may rest with them in the kingdom of my Father." Three months later the Lord chastised them for "fearing man," and gave them specific counsel to go forth to preach, not fearing what man could do to them.

Other men who came to the Prophet in the months following the organization of the Church in April 1830 were Hyrum, Samuel and Joseph Smith Sr., and Parley Pratt, who received personal revelations and stayed the course; but others who also received personal revelations regarding their **duty** included Thomas Marsh and Sidney Rigdon, who labored well but failed to endure in their **duties.**

James Covill covenanted that he would obey any command that the Lord would give to him through Joseph the Prophet, which resulted in his receiving a wonderful promise in D&C 39. The Prophet reported several days later that Covill had rejected the word of the Lord and had returned to his former principles and people; and the Lord revealed in D&C 40 that Covill "received the word with gladness, but straightway Satan tempted him; and the fear of persecution and the cares of the world caused him to reject the word. Wherefore, he broke my covenant, and it remaineth with me to do with him as seemeth me good."

The Lord gave a revelation to Joseph Smith on July 23, 1837, instructing Thomas Marsh as President of the Twelve to teach the members of the Twelve regarding their **duty** and responsibilities in proclaiming the Gospel. At this time, some of the apostles had forsaken their **duties** and had turned their attention to speculative pursuits. This revelation was a warning to him and a call for him to bring his brethren back to their **duties** as apostles of Jesus Christ.

The conspiracy that developed following the failure of the Kirtland Safety Society bank caused much confusion and doubt among many of the leaders of the Church. They either abandoned their exalted **duties** in the priesthood councils to speculative pursuits or to seek to overthrow Joseph Smith and his supporters in Kirtland. Those who lost their way, when they endeavored to cover their sins by accusing Joseph to be a fallen prophet, lost the Holy Spirit and the confidence of the faithful. These dissidents, who became apostates, included apostles John Boynton, Luke and Lyman Johnson, and William McLellin, as well as Warren Parrish and other men who had served faithfully until this severe test of their faith. These men and dozens of others were either excommunicated or just left the Church. Once they ceased to serve in the **duties** they had accepted, they fell into apostasy and became active conspirators in destroying the Prophet Joseph and the Church of Jesus Christ.

> It was a sorrowful day for Joseph when he lost the companionship of these men who had been with him during many trials and who had participated with him in the glorious understanding of heavenly

things. But they were no longer anything but dead branches, harmful to the growing tree, and it was necessary for the pruner to lop them off. . . . It was sad to see them thus shorn of power and blessing, but they had demonstrated their unworthiness to hold the positions which they had filled.

Had Joseph's faith in God and confidence in the mission which the Creator had entrusted to him been less than it was, he might have temporized with these men and not dealt with them in so strict and summary a manner. He was attached to them by many ties. . . . However much, then, Joseph's affection and friendship might be for these men, he owed a paramount **duty** to his God to deal with transgressors in His Church according to the laws which He had given (George Q. Cannon, *Life of Joseph Smith the Prophet*, 239).

One of the most infamous breaches of trust and **duty** came at Far West, when the Saints were under siege by the Missouri Militia under General Lucas. The ranking Mormon officer, Lt. Colonel George Hinkle met with General Lucas to discuss an arrangement to permit the Saints to avoid armed conflict with the state troops and the various mobs in the area.

Colonel Hinkle returned to Far West and reported to Joseph Smith that the officers of the militia desired to have an interview with him and some others—naming those stipulated by General Lucas—hoping that the difficulties might be settled without carrying into effect the governor's Exterminating Orders. To this "interview," the brethren named readily assented, but to their surprise, on meeting General Lucas and the troops that came forward from the main body to receive them, Colonel Hinkle said: "General, these are the prisoners I agreed to deliver up." They were then surrounded and marched off as prisoners. On reaching the enemy's encampment . . . the prisoners lay in the open air with nothing as a covering, and they were all drenched with rain before morning. All night long they were mocked and taunted by the guard, who

> demanded signs, saying, "Come Mr. Smith, show us
> an angel, give us some of your revelations, show us a
> miracle;" mingling these requests with the vilest
> oaths . . . obscenity . . . deeds of rapine and murder,
> and boast of their conquest over virtuous wives and
> maidens by brute force (B. H. Roberts, *Comprehensive
> History of the Church*, 1:486).

Following their arrest at Far West, Joseph and others
were tried and sentenced to the filthy jail in Liberty, Missouri. "Sidney Rigdon, according to a generally prevailing
impression, was more or less, under the influence of a spirit
of apostasy. It is related that, in Liberty jail, he declared to
his fellow-prisoners that the sufferings of the Lord were
nothing compared with his, and while the faithful Saints
were straining every nerve to complete their leave from
Missouri, he had no word of encouragement to them. As a
consequence of his disposition, he did not have good
health. Like the Corinthians who partook unworthily of the
Sacrament (I Cor. 11:3), he was 'weak and sickly.' The Lord,
therefore, points out to him the cause of his ailments and
promises to heal him, if he will do his **duty** and stand by the
Prophet as a true counselor" (Hyrum M. Smith and Janne M.
Sjodahl, *Doctrine and Covenants Commentary*, 788).

Sometimes we are given many opportunities to exercise our **duties**. Such was the case with Apostle John E.
Page. When he was called to a mission to Canada, he
refused because he was destitute of clothing, so Joseph
Smith gave him his coat and a promise that the Lord would
bless him. In two years John baptized 600 souls. Following
his ordination as an apostle in July 1838, he failed to join
members of the Twelve in their great mission to England.
Soon after, he was called but failed to go with Orson Hyde
to dedicate Palestine for the return of the Jews. Two years
later, John and fellow apostles organized the Saints in
Cincinnati; however, John stayed behind and overruled

what had been done. Despite John's repeated failures to magnify his high calling, he was sustained as an apostle, until finally he ceased to perform his apostolic **duties**.

Another apostle who began in a most promising manner, but then appeared like a falling comet, was William Smith, the younger brother of the Prophet. After earlier successes as a missionary, William failed to join the Twelve in 1840 on their mission to England, giving poverty as an excuse. The following spring he visited branches of the Church in the East, where he collected monies from the members for his own use. On one occasion, he physically attacked the Prophet over a difference of opinion. Finally, he was rejected by the Twelve for womanizing, lying, physical injuring and maligning the Prophet, retaining monies raised for Church offerings, and preaching against Brigham Young.

In every situation failure to perform our **duties** causes the loss of the spirit. When we lose the spirit, and know that we have failed in our **duty**, the adversary can provide us with a myriad of excuses to withdraw from activity and to criticize Church leaders and others.

The fall from grace and authority of church leaders, including bishops and others in local wards and branches, is a great calamity, causing some members to question the councils of the Church or the depth of their own personal testimony. President Harold B. Lee warned us repeatedly to gain our own testimony of the gospel and not rely on the borrowed light of others.

One of the great tragedies today in the Church, as in earlier times, is the loss of new converts. We, and they, have not understood well the necessity of their gaining greater knowledge and conviction of the doctrine, and their **duty** to pursue a full understanding of gospel principles and the priesthood ordinances and blessings. We have the **duty** to help them become united with us in the fullness of saintly performance. They have the **duty** to take hold of the iron rod and walk resolutely forward to the tree of life, which requires study, prayer, service, and conformance to all of the **duties** and commandments that are part of the baptismal and the everlasting covenants.

If we are to be faithful and enduring in our lives, and especially so individually and in our families, we have the **duty** to discover what the Lord expects of us. Simply, it involves the following:

- we must know our **duty**
- we must determine **what we need to do** to perform our **duty**
- **seek help** to do it
- **do it**, as President Spencer W. Kimball counseled us

As Zion's Camp reached Fishing River en route to rescue the Saints in Missouri in June 1834, the Lord revealed to the Prophet that "they should wait for a season, because the Church, not individuals, was in transgression. . . . They have not learned to be obedient to the things which I required at their hands . . . do not impart of their substance, as becometh saints, to the poor and afflicted among them . . . that my people may be taught more perfectly . . . and **know** more perfectly concerning their **duty**, and the things which I require at their hands" (D&C 105:2,3, 10).

> The most advanced, universal, and practical leadership philosophy ever put forth was given in this simple statement by the Prophet Joseph Smith: "I teach the people correct principles and they govern themselves" (John Taylor, *Journal of Discourses*, 10:57–58). [1862]

> Area Presidencies are to teach stake presidencies the overall vision, direction, purpose, and correct principles of the Church, and then they are to let stake

presidents govern or manage their stakes. A similar pattern applies to bishops and their wards and to parents and their families. "Wherefore, now let every man learn his **duty**, and to act in the office in which he is appointed, in all diligence (D&C 107:99) (M. Russell Ballard, *Counseling with Our Councils*, 58–59).

President Ezra Taft Benson taught that it is an obligation of parents to see that these sacred ordinances are performed after the children have been properly taught. It is not the prerogative of parents to permit their children to grow up and choose for themselves. It is their **duty** and obligation to train them when they are yet young, and to see that these important ordinances are performed in their behalf (Ezra Taft Benson, *So Shall Ye Reap*, 111).

President Marion G. Romney was a great proponent of the needs and responsibilities of individuals:

> We must see to it that everyone who needs help has the opportunity and, to the extent of his power, does do all he can to obtain for himself what he needs.
>
> In addition to each person's responsibility to take care of his own needs, husbands have a divinely imposed **duty** to support their wives. "Women," says the Lord, "have claim on their husbands for their maintenance, until their husbands are taken . . ." (D&C 83:2).
>
> Parents likewise have a responsibility to care for their children. . . . In this dispensation the Lord has said, "All children have claim upon their parents for their maintenance until they are of age" (D&C 83:4).
>
> The next responsibility I wish to call to mind is the **duty** of children to care for their parents. Since this obligation is often observed in the breach, and since the rewards for observing it are so great and the penalty for disregarding it so severe. . . . "Honor thy father and thy mother: that thy days may be long upon the land which the Lord thy God giveth thee" (Marion G. Romney, *Learning for the Eternities*, 202).

Elder Henry B. Eyring speaks from our time but in words as timeless as the patriarchs of old:

> Parents have a sacred **duty** to rear their children in love and righteousness, to provide for their physical and spiritual needs, to teach them to love and serve one another, to observe the commandments of God and to be law-abiding citizens wherever they live. Husbands and wives—mothers and fathers—will be held accountable before God for the discharge of these obligations.
>
> The family is ordained of God. Marriage between man and woman is essential to His eternal plan. Children are entitled to birth within the bonds of matrimony, and to be reared by a father and mother who honor marital vows with complete fidelity. . . . Successful marriages and families are established and maintained on principles of faith, prayer, repentance, forgiveness, respect, love, compassion, work, and wholesome recreational activities. By divine design, fathers are to provide the necessities of life and protection for their families. Mothers are primarily responsible for the nurture of their children. In these sacred responsibilities, fathers and mothers are obligated to help one another as equal partners. Disability, death, or other circumstances may necessitate individual adaptation. Extended families should lend support when needed (Henry B. Eyring, *To Draw Closer to God*, 166).

As we try to prepare our children for their future in a wicked world, we are entitled to call upon the Father of our spirits, who loves us beyond our comprehension, to help us know what to say and do. It requires that we be able to receive his assistance, which will normally come through promptings from the Holy Ghost to those who are worthy to hear his quiet voice. It may also reach us through others who love us and/or have a **duty** to care for us, i.e., a bishop, a home and visiting teacher, or a relative or friend.

The Savior's invitation is that we "ask, and it shall

be given you; seek, and ye shall find; knock, and it shall be opened unto you. For every one that asketh receiveth; and he that seeketh findeth; and to him that knocketh it shall be opened" (Matt. 6:7–8).

> The Lord revealed himself and his Son Jesus Christ to the Prophet Joseph in answer to the latter's earnest prayer to know the truth respecting the various religions; Moroni came three years later in response to the young Prophet's earnest prayer to know his standing before the Lord; nearly all the early revelations to individuals in the church, to Joseph Smith, Sen., Hyrum Smith, Oliver Cowdery, Joseph Knight, Sen., David, Peter, John and Christian Whitmer, were given in answer to the inquiry of these men to know their **duty** in respect of the work of the Lord (B. H. Roberts, *Comprehensive History of the Church*, 1:379).

Elder Gene R. Cook testified: "I bear testimony that the Lord fulfills his promises. If we will do our part, be patient, and keep the commandments, the Lord will answer our prayers concerning our families. He will bless us in our *sacred duty* to raise up our children unto him" (Gene R. Cook, *Raising up a Child unto the Lord*, xxvii).

To protect us and those we love from the horrors of apostasy, we must learn our **duty** to God, our families, and the Church. This knowledge needs to be imparted to those for whom we are responsible so that we can strive in unity to obey. Because of the power and skill of the adversary, we must have the faith and direction of the Holy Spirit to help us to walk the straight and narrow path to the tree of life. And finally, we must follow the words and practices of righteousness that we can find our way through the worldly minefield that accosts us at every hour and place.

It is in our homes, chapels and in the temples that we are safe from the wiles of the devil and the enticements of the world, if we learn our **duty** and **do** it.

Don't Heed Revelation

The plan of salvation has been revealed to the children of a loving Heavenly Father in all ages of mankind. Some of this **revelation** is found in the holy scriptures, but the great portion is unrecorded; although we are fortunate to have oral tradition and personal journals and records that bless the lives of the faithful. Privileged are those who have ancestors who have recorded the **inspiration** and testimony they enjoyed as they endured the trials of life and the blessings that came to them.

On the contrary, how tragic are the descendants of those who did not heed the **scriptures,** the **counsel** from God's servants, or the **personal revelation** that was given for their guidance and encouragement. Unfortunately, pride, fear, worldly cares and a host of other influences that the adversary promotes, have caused confusion in the wayward, as well as among the faithful.

Apostle John A. Widstoe wrote that there are two basic types of **revelation**: (1) those given to individuals, and (2) those given to the Church for doctrinal information, for organizational purposes, and those dealing with miscellaneous subjects (John A. Widstoe, *The Message of the Doctrine and Covenants*, 4–9).

The Doctrine and Covenants contains many personal **warnings** to the early Saints, including the Prophet, regarding their duties, sins and weaknesses. The Prophet Joseph was directed by the Spirit to chastise and instruct individuals as well as the saints in general.

Today, we are blessed with counsel, both oral and written, from Church leaders regarding the dangers of living in a wicked world and the blessings of righteous living. But most beneficent are the personal **promptings** of the Holy Spirit which may come to us in many ways but, most wonderfully, in answer to our prayers that seek specific direction.

Relating to the loss of the 116 pages of manuscript translated from the gold plates, that had been given to Martin Harris, the Lord reminded Joseph Smith in July 1828, "For although a man may have many **revelations,** and have power to do many mighty works, yet if he boasts in his own strength, and sets at naught the counsels of God, and follows after the dictates of his own will and carnal desires, he must fall and incur the vengeance of a just God upon him. . . . For, behold, you should not have feared man more than God . . . if thou are not aware thou wilt fall" (D&C 3:4, 9).

When Hyrum Smith desired to know what he should be about in May 1829, the Lord told him: "Now, as you have asked, behold, I say unto you, keep my commandments, and seek to bring forth and establish the cause of Zion. . . . Deny not the spirit of **revelation**" (D&C 11:6, 25).

Three years later in Jackson County, Missouri, the Prophet received a **revelation** which chastised the Saints, "even all of you have sinned," and then reminded them: "Ye call upon my name for **revelations,** and I give them unto you; and inasmuch as ye keep not my sayings, which I give unto you, ye become transgressors; and justice and judgment are the penalty which is affixed unto my law. . . . Watch, for the adversary spreadeth his dominions, and darkness reigneth" (D&C 82:4–5).

> At the inception of mob action in Jackson County, Missouri, the Lord counseled the saints and instructed them in the course of action they should pursue (see D&C sections 97 and 98). Many did not

heed His counsel. Had they been obedient and followed His instructions they would never have been driven out of Jackson County.

Approximately six weeks after the saints were driven from the county, the Lord gave to His prophet, a **revelation** (D&C 101) explaining why the expulsion of the saints. He also counseled them concerning the redemption of Zion and the promises that would be fulfilled concerning Zion at His second coming and during His millennial reign (Otten and Caldwell, *Sacred Truths of the Doctrine and Covenants*, 2:208).

In the Lord's preface to the Doctrine and Covenants, He says, "And the arm of the Lord shall be revealed; and the day cometh that they who will not hear the voice of the Lord, neither the voice of his servants, neither give heed to the **words of the prophets and apostles,** shall be cut off from among the people; For they have strayed from my ordinances, and have broken mine everlasting covenant; They seek not the Lord to establish his righteousness, but every man walketh in his own way" (D&C 1:14–16).

William E. McLellin became prominent in the early Church. He was at one time a member of the first Council of Twelve Apostles. On October 25, 1831, he received a marvelous **revelation** through the Prophet Joseph:

> Ye are clean, but not all; repent, therefore, of those things which are not pleasing in my sight. . . . Proclaim my gospel from land to land. . . . Lay your hands upon the sick, and they shall recover. . . . Ask, and ye shall receive; knock, and it shall be opened unto you. . . . **Keep these sayings,** for they are true and faithful; and thou shalt magnify thine office. . . . Continue in these things even unto the end, and you shall have a crown of eternal life at the right hand of my Father. . . (D&C 66:2, 5, 9, 11, 12).

However, unfortunately for him, he did not heed the warning given in this **revelation**. He fell, and on

May 11, 1838, he was severed from the Church at Far West (Hyrum M. Smith and Janne M. Sjodahl, *Doctrine and Covenants Commentary*, 402).

Recall that Hiram Page obtained a stone through which he received a **revelation** as to the location of Zion, which captured the belief of Oliver Cowdery and the Whitmer family. In D&C 30 the Lord chastises David Whitmer for succumbing to this **false revelation,** which came from an unauthorized source.

After the Church had been established in the West, a crises arose in the mid-1850s. "Its root cause was a change of focus. At first the Saints aimed to build a model society. Along the way, however, the focus of many changed to wealth, comfortable homes, and security, which appear to have become more important than creating an ensign to the nations. With that change among the Saints came a careless attitude toward their religion. Sabbath breaking, profanity, and sexual immorality crept in.

> Viewing this condition with alarm, President Young decided a strong antidote was necessary. His remedy was to launch what became known as "**the Reformation.**" It was a call to repentance. President Young told them, "I cannot hold men and women in fellowship that serve the devil and themselves, and give no heed to the Almighty. . . . You must part with your sins . . ." This kind of straight talk had a bracing effect on most of the Saints who had strayed. They were rebaptized as a symbol of their repentance and returned to their obedient ways. However, a few left the territory, unwilling to live up to so strict a standard, while others remained to become sour dissidents, opposed to the Church and its leaders (Francis M. Gibbons, *Dynamic Disciples*, 49).

Apostle Amasa Lyman had performed so faithfully numerous missions and many dangerous errands. Then while he was Mission President in London, Amasa preached in Dundee, Scotland, that the Savior was only a "holy man" and that the atonement was not necessary. After confessing his error of such a critical doctrine to the Twelve, he fell errant again after he returned to Utah. He became involved in spiritualism, in a movement that entertained seances and visits from departed persons from the spirit world. Amasa accepted instructions and guidance from these spiritual manifestations, contrary to the **scriptures** and the **counsel** from the leaders of the Church. He died apostate, not recognizing nor desiring the guidance of the Holy Spirit.

President George Q. Cannon describes the fate of those who deny their covenants and the inspiration that they had once enjoyed:

> Every apostate from the truth, Judas-like, indulges in this same feeling; and the hatred which they bear to the principles they once rejoiced in and its believers, their former brethren, is varied in intensity by the progress they made in the knowledge of truth when they loved it and the extent to which they abandon themselves to the influence which their master exercises. . . .
>
> When a man obeys the truth, or the Gospel of Jesus Christ, which comprehends all truth, he receives a spirit of light and intelligence, of peace and joy; he has a foretaste, as it were, of heaven. If he cherish it, it will increase within him and continually afford him the purest happiness, will fill him with peace and good-will to men and gradually lead him into all truth. But if he grieve and quench it after having once enjoyed it, it will decrease within him, until he will be entirely destitute of it and a prey to exactly the opposite feelings to those produced by its presence. He will hate the truth as strongly as he formerly loved it, and he will wonder how he could ever see anything about it that was lovely or attractive. Hence, Satan does not have the power over men who never knew the truth that he does over those who apostatize therefrom (George Q. Cannon, *Gospel Truth*, 496–97).

One of the reasons people apostatize from this Church is that they have failed to heed the warning of the **scriptures** against listening to false teachers who raise their voices in our midst. In spite of the fact that these warnings of the **scriptures** are crystal clear, many of our people fail to heed them. . . . They (teachers) do so by attacking the fundamental doctrines of the Church. They attack the teachings of the Authorities. . . . Remember, too, the Savior told the Prophet Joseph Smith that it is Satan who 'doth stir up the fears of the people to contention concerning the points of doctrine (Mark E. Petersen, *Conference Report,* October 1945).

You will note the apostle said: ". . . whereunto ye do well that ye take heed," referring to prophecy. His **words** are as applicable today as they were then. Students of prophecy and history find that, in general, people have not taken heed. It is particularly noticeable that the generations to whom prophecies of old had special application, that is to say, the people who lived in the days when the prophecies were being fulfilled, ordinarily were unmindful of that fact, unable to interpret the prophecies in the light of current events, or current events in the light of prophecy (Hugh B. Brown, *Continuing the Quest,* 337).

Thousands of new members have built upon the foundation of their faith at the time of their baptism, but there are wolves in sheep's clothing among them. Older members by bad example could wound their weak conscience, and make their weaker brethren to offend. [See 1 Cor. 8:11–13] Dissension and confusion could result from lack of experience, and the tide of persecution from the outside could roll in upon them and engulf them in a flood of apostasy unless they **heed the Lord's warnings** (Harold B. Lee, *Stand Ye in Holy Places,* 201).

As the missionaries brought increasing numbers of converts into the early Church, these converts brought with them many of their former beliefs and traditions with them. Many of these beliefs were cherished by the converts, so that it was not surprising that they would occasionally come in conflict with Church doctrine and directions from Church leaders.

> Members of the Church have no difficulty following and giving heed to the words of the prophet as long as he says that which agrees with their views. The problems arise when the prophet issues statements that conflict with the opinion of some members. They seemingly forget their differences do not lie with the prophet, but rather with the Lord himself. The Savior directed: "For his **word** (the prophet) ye shall receive, as if from mine own mouth, in all patience and faith" (D&C 21:5).

> When the Lord uses the word "patience," a time period is involved. Though we may not now see the full implications of the prophet's message, time will exonerate his word. In the meantime, while seeking for complete understanding, we are counseled to have "faith" sufficient to act on the Lord's words given through His prophet (L. G. Otten and C. M. Caldwell, *Sacred Truths of the Doctrine and Covenants*, 92).

President Marion G. Romney said: "It is an easy thing to believe in the dead prophets, but it is a greater thing to believe in the living prophets."

President Joseph Fielding Smith observed that there are

> too many who will not heed the counsels that are given in the **revelations** of the Lord, notwithstanding the magnitude of the promised blessings. There have been some who feel, as President John Taylor expressed: "who think that they can slide into the kingdom of God," without complying with the commandments. By this he meant that they expect to receive the blessings of exaltation because their names are still on the records of the Church; but they have not prepared themselves by active participation in

faithful performance of duty (Joseph Fielding Smith, *Answers to Gospel Questions,* 2:xii).

Whereas the early Saints were tried in ways that we find fearful—pillaging, rape, beatings, spoliation, betrayal, our trials are more subtle and devious. The devil and his agents have perverted morals standards and entertainment media, so that the faithful must be ever alert and pro active in dealing with people and institutions that occupy our time, resources and attention. Above all, we need the discernment that comes from understanding the difference between good and evil, and the ability to apply this understanding to the challenges we face daily.

Where can we obtain this capacity to know what we should do and say?

Four sources seem especially helpful for those who desire to avoid the fate of those whom we have cited above and in the profiles of apostate members:

- Familiarity with the **scriptures, messages** in the *Ensign* and other church publications, and general conference **sermons**
- **Attendance** in the temples and church meetings, especially Sacrament meeting
- Daily personal and family **prayer**
- Retaining the **Holy Spirit,** which requires repentance and obedience to covenants and commandments

These sources, when followed, will qualify us for the **direction** of the Spirit. But we must learn to recognize its promptings, which may be in a "still, small voice," that must compete with the multitude of "voices" that assail us at work, at home and at other worldly places. We can arm ourselves with the language of truth by reading the **scriptures** and hearing the **words of our inspired leaders.** Then when we pray and wait upon the Lord for guidance, we will be able to recognize the heavenly words and ideas that are conveyed to us. But it is the Spirit that permits our spirit, our intellect, to comprehend the true and full meaning of what we should do and say.

President Harold B. Lee spoke of the necessity of possessing the Spirit in understanding the counsel of Church leaders:

> I had heard the **warnings** of these and other unpleasant conditions that would result when the Spirit of the Lord was withdrawn because of transgression. The **warnings** have been given many times by the General Authorities as they have come to our meetings to **counsel** us. How often I failed to heed their warning!
>
> Now I am being taught the correctness of their words by the most costly of all teachers, experience. I know that their **warnings** were inspired. I know now that the conditions they said would follow in the darkness that comes with the loss of the Spirit to transgressors were as sure as the night follows the day. I add my warning, as one who is being taught by sorrowful, costly experience, to that of the leaders and give testimony that they know whereof they speak. It is given in hope that someone will be moved to heed the **counsel** of these wise men before he too has regrets that cannot be overcome and sorrows that cannot be assuaged (Harold B. Lee, *Stand Ye in Holy Places*, 120).

President Lee explained the role of the Church in instructing and blessing its members in these "last days":

> The place of the Church in preserving truth in these "the latter times" is thus pointed out when "some shall depart from the faith, giving heed to seducing spirits, and doctrines of devils; speaking lies in hypocrisy; having their conscience seared with a hot iron, forbidding to marry and commanding to abstain from meat . . ." (1 Timothy 4:1–3).

So the Church of Jesus Christ declares with a boldness that is always characteristic of truth: "We believe all that God **has revealed**, all that he does **now reveal**, and we believe that he will **yet reveal** many great and important things pertaining to the kingdom of God." [A of F 9] And again ". . . We believe all things, we hope all things. . . . If there is anything virtuous, lovely, or of good report or praiseworthy, we seek after these things." [A of F 13] Indeed the Church of Jesus Christ does not ask you to give up any truth that you may learn from science or philosophy, law or medicine. Rather is the Church commanded:

". . . that you may be instructed more perfectly in theory, in principle, in doctrine, in the law of the gospel, in all things that pertain unto the kingdom of God, that are expedient for you to understand; of things both in heaven and in the earth, and under the earth; things which have been, things which are; things which must shortly come to pass, things which are at home, things which are abroad; the wars and perplexities of the nations, and judgments which are on the land; and a knowledge also of countries and of kingdoms" (D&C 88:78–79) (Harold B. Lee, *Decisions for Successful Living*, 191).

There are some members of the Church who seemingly complain because the Lord is not giving **revelations** to be placed in the Doctrine and Covenants as in the beginning and ask why **revelation** has ceased in the Church. Usually it is the case that these critics are not faithfully keeping the commandments the Lord has already given and their eyes are blind to the fact that **revelation** and the guidance of the Lord is being meted out to the Church constantly (Joseph Fielding Smith, *Church History and Modern Revelation*, p. 53).

President Smith explained further: "Let us one and all take an inward look. Perhaps it is because we have not humbled ourselves, because we have failed to heed the commandments and to accept and abide in the **revelations** already given, that there is not more given to us. It is my humble opinion that we are receiving council by **inspiration,** or **revelation,** at every general conference of the Church. Would it not be wise for the members of the Church to pay more **heed to these counsels** and prepare ourselves for more to come?" (Joseph Fielding Smith, *Answers to Gospel Questions,* 2:205).

> More than once the Lord simply says you will need to hear his voice, but you will need to hear his voice from him and from his servants. "And the arm of the Lord shall be **revealed**; and the day cometh that they who will not hear the voice of the Lord, neither the voice of his servants, neither give heed to the words of the prophets and apostles, shall be cut off from among the people."
>
> I know a few of the reasons why the Lord requires us to listen to mortal servants. One of the reasons is that you and I need a check on our own inspiration occasionally. We can be mistaken. At times, even with real intent and with faith and with careful prayer, we may come to wrong conclusions. Listening to others can provide correction. It can promote more careful consideration. I hope you will always remember that there is safety in **counsel** (Henry B. Eyring, *To Draw Closer to God,* 11).

President Joseph Fielding Smith counsels that we must be patient in our pursuit of perfection:

> We consider that God has created man with a mind capable of instruction, and a faculty which may be enlarged in proportion to the heed and diligence given to the light communicated from heaven to the intellect; and that the nearer man approaches perfection, the clearer are his views, and the greater his enjoyments, till he has overcome the evils of his life and lost every desire for sin. . . . But we consider that this is a station to which no man ever arrived in a

moment; he must have been instructed in the government and laws of that kingdom by proper degrees (Joseph Fielding Smith, *Take Heed to Yourselves*, 5).

In our day, the Lord has counseled many times, **"Pray always"** (see D&C 19:28; 32:4; 75:11 88:126; 93:49). In this latter reference, the Lord tells us: "What I say unto one I say unto all; **pray always** lest that wicked one have power in you, and remove out of your place."

Unfortunately, Martin Harris, Luke Johnson, William McLellin did not follow this counsel and were cut off from the influence of the Spirit and from their holy callings.

George Q. Cannon, evidently speaking from personal experience, speaks movingly about the benefits of **prayer**:

> **Prayer** is an unfailing source of happiness. It is a continued cause of relief to those who offer it in a proper spirit to the Most High. The burdened and afflicted soul who goes to the Lord in prayer never comes away without relief. Those who are tempted and tried do not seek Him in vain, when they bow themselves before Him. How anyone calling himself a Latter-day Saint can neglect this duty, which is so productive of benefits, which brings so much comfort and increases joy so materially, which is a source of strength and a safeguard against every evil, is most strange. Whenever **prayer** is neglected, it is evident that faith is lacking; whether the person who neglects it has never known the blessings which result from it or, if he has known them, has so far forgotten the goodness of God as to be in a most dangerous condition.
>
> However faithful men and women may be, they still are required to watch and **pray**; for they are commanded, 'Let him that thinketh he standeth take heed lest he fall' (1 Corinthians 10:12). But the man or the woman who does not pray is positively unsafe and is liable to be overcome at any moment and to become an alien to all the covenants and promises of the Lord (George Q. Cannon, *Gospel Truths*, 410).

Apostle John A. Widstoe declared: "When apostasy comes, it is because the spirit of **revelation** departs from us. The wire is broken between us and the source of truth. We cannot understand, though truth be spoken, since we are not possessed of the spirit of truth. We misunderstand and misinterpret" (John A. Widstoe, *Conference Report*, October 1934).

The **scriptures and counsel from living prophets** provide us with general guidance to righteous behavior. But it is **personal revelation,** especially in answers to our specific prayers, that will protect and teach us the way to peace, righteousness and joy.

AMBITION

Something fascinates the American public with being Number One. Hugh Nibley has noted that many of us would rather be Number One in hell than a doorkeeper in the Houses of the Lord. Or, as Satan put it in Milton's *Paradise Lost*, "To reign is worth **ambition.** Better to reign in Hell than to serve in Heaven" (Bruce C. Hafen, *The Broken Heart*, 93).

Ambition for power, adulation, a place in history, or worldly things attracts many of us. If our goal is to bless the lives of the poor and the needy, we may enjoy the approbation of the Lord and the companionship of the Spirit. However, if we are motivated by the glorification and indulgence of ourselves, we may expect to battle for our position by our own wits and energy, and that of anyone we can enlist in our cause. Competition is always before us, because there are always others, men or women, who want our place.

But we must be aware, lest we succumb to the dangers that Lord Acton warns, that "power tends to corrupt, and absolute power corrupts absolutely."

Apostle John A. Widstoe identifies for us the ultimate practitioner of **ambition**—Satan:

The story of Lucifer is the most terrible example of such apostasy. Lucifer, son of the morning, through diligent search for truth and the use of it, had become one of the foremost in the assembly of those invited to undertake the experiences of earth. But, in that Great

Council, his personal **ambition** and love of power overcame him. He pitted his own plan and will against the
purposes of God. He strove to gain the birthright of
his Elder Brother, Jesus the Christ. When his proposi-
tion was rejected, he forsook all that he had gained,
would not repent of his sin, defied truth, and of necessity lost his place among the followers of God. He was
no longer Lucifer, bearer of truth, who walked in light,
but Satan, teacher of untruth, who slunk in darkness.

He became the enemy of God and of all who try
to walk according to the Lord's commandments. One-
third of the spirits present in that vast assembly sup-
ported Satan and became enemies of the truth that
they had formerly cherished. With him these rebellious spirits lost their fellowship with the valiant sons
of God. What is more, they lost the privilege of obtaining bodies of flesh and blood, without which they
cannot gain full power over the forces of the universe.
In the face of that defeat, and that curse, they have
sought from Adam to the present time to corrupt
mankind and defeat the Lord's purposes (John A.
Widstoe, *Evidences and Reconciliations*, 209).

An example of the insidious nature of **ambition** is
found in Shakespeare's *Macbeth*, wherein a little hint of
the glory of power and prestige can lead to monstrous acts
and destruction:

In *Macbeth*, Shakespeare portrays a man in
whom the worm of **ambition**, of greed for power,
steadily grows until it leads to his destruction. When
told by the three witches that he will be king hereafter,
Macbeth first demurs, insisting he has no **ambitions**.
But the worm begins to grow, and soon Macbeth is
plotting murder, vacillating between willingness to
kill Duncan the king and momentary shrinking from
the dreadful deed. "If it were done, when 'tis done,
then 'twere well / It were done quickly," he muses.
Then drawing back from the increasingly delicious
contemplation of evil, he piously proclaims that Duncan is here in double trust: / first, as I am his kinsman

and his kinsman and his subject, / Strong both against the deed; then, as his host, / who should against his murderer shut the door, /not bear the knife myself." Urged on by his avaricious wife ("screw your courage to the sticking-place, / And we'll not fail"), Macbeth succumbs to evil, and the devil leads him thenceforth. Shakespeare's genius portrays the triumph of evil in a man who did not start out bad but ended up with "his secret murders sticking on his hands."

The lesson of the play—that **ambition** for power and the improper use of power corrupts and ultimately destroys—is universal and applicable in all societies and in every period of history" (Alexander Morrison, *Feed My Sheep*, 170).

Men of great **ambition** abound in the scriptures: Cain, Gadianton, Kishkumen, Herod, Gidianhi, Nebuchadnezzar. But the men who were most devious and vindictive were they who had been enlightened by the word of God and then turned to evil and the pursuit of power over those who had been their brethren. Among these **ambitious** seekers was a Nephite named Amalikiah:

The rebels were led by a descendant of Zoram, the servant of Laban, named Amalikiah, one of the most ambitious, cunning, and unscrupulous characters that ever disgraced the history of ancient America. It was a perilous day for the Nephite Nation when this subtle creature bent all his brilliant energies to the fulfillment of his **ambitious** dreams. True, he had been a member of Christ's holy Church, but now the love of God had given place to the hatred of His servants; he was a citizen of a republic, but he aspired to overthrow its liberties and reign as king over his fellowmen. Indeed he had cherished thoughts of still greater power, even to be monarch of the entire continent; both Nephite and Lamanite should bow to his undisputed sway. Such were his dreams, and the continual thoughts of his waking hours, and to this end he bent all the energies of his mind, all the craft of his soul, all the cunning of his tongue, all the weight of his influence.

With promises rich as gold and numerous as snow-flakes in a winter's storm, he beguiled his weaker fellows; men, who like him, loved power, hated the truth, delighted in iniquity, but who had not the lofty **ambition**, the unhallowed valor, and the deep designing cunning that distinguished their leader. To his call the dissatisfied, the corrupt and the apostate rallied.

That the corruption sown by one wicked man may yield a harvest of misery and woe to a nation or to any number of individuals is amply shown in the experiences of Amalikiah. He even sought to destroy God's Church, and not only that, but to bring to naught the government of the people which "God had granted to them (George Reynolds and Janne M. Sjodahl, *Commentary on the Book of Mormon*, 5:38).

As the Lord readied the events leading to the restoration of all things, it was certain that men and women would come forth to shoulder the burdens of this glorious undertaking. There would be men of valor and faithfulness, and those doing the bidding of Satan to oppose the work. The mighty gifts of the Spirit were manifest from the First Vision and throughout the glorious days of the restoration of the priesthood, the gospel, the Book of Mormon, and the missionary labors.

The great Prophet of the latter days, Joseph Smith, stood at the vortex of the flood of revelation, organization, and zealous activity that began in 1827, when the angel Moroni delivered the gold plates, and continued for almost two decades. Commencing at the First Vision in 1823, and continuing on to our day, Satan has striven to destroy the work of God. While opposition and persecution was mounted by sectarian ministers and various governmental entities, the most damaging hostility came from apostates who had enjoyed the spiritual gifts and the blessings of communion with the Saints. This unrelenting opposition was directed at the Prophet.

But the Lord, his angels, his immediate family, and the Holy Spirit had prepared Joseph well to endure the persecution and the duties of bringing forth the Church of Christ. Historian Edward Tullidge has described well some of the qualities of the Man:

> The grandeur of Joseph's character is most shown in his lack of pretension. Christ declared Himself the head of the Church; and though Joseph was to be our Savior's representative here on earth, he exacted no homage from his fellow believers, but only such respect as the gospel required them to pay. The thought of gaining glory for himself appears never to have entered his mind. His conduct in the beginning, in execution of the requirements of the Lord, was a type of his whole life. The commands of God came through him to earth, and he gave them voice firmly and fearlessly. Speaking as a prophet of God under the influence of the spirit, he brooked no opposition; but in his personal relations with his fellow apostles and elders he gave them, according to their station and their desserts, as much deference as he asked, or was willing to receive for himself. This characteristic gave him power in the beginning. Only he who knows how to obey is worthy to command; only he who yields to others their due can expect compliance with his own order, however lawful it may be (Edward W. Tullidge, *Life of Joseph the Prophet*, 80).

The faithful would draw from the greatness of the prophet to magnify their souls and the callings that were given them. But Joseph's youth, lack of education and experience in worldly affairs caused many converts to reason that their qualifications made them superior to him. Such **ambitious** thoughts were accentuated when Joseph made some mistakes, or others did not fully understand what Joseph, or the Lord through Joseph, had spoken. Such occasions beguiled many of Joseph's closest and greatest associates in the ministry. **Ambition** overcame Oliver Cowdery, Sidney Rigdon, David Whitmer, John C. Bennett, William Law, Thomas Marsh, Warren Parrish, and others.

> About the time Elder Pratt reached Nauvoo, Sidney Rigdon, one of the counselors to the martyred Prophet, arrived from Pennsylvania. He was invited to join them (Twelve Apostles) in their movements, but he declined, as he had his own selfish **ambition** to gratify. He was determined to become the leader of the Church; and to accomplish this, he began in an underhanded way to work up a feeling in his favor.
>
> He held secret meetings among those favorable to this plans, circulated wonderful "revelations" among them, and ordained men to offices heretofore unheard of in the Church. . . . Elder Rigdon had full opportunity to present his claims to the people, but they rejected him. . . . Disappointed in his **ambitious** designs, Elder Rigdon sought to divide the people; but as his influence in Nauvoo was limited. . . .
>
> Other restless, **ambitious** characters, among them James J. Strang and James Emmet sought to divide the Church, since they could not preside over it, and did lead some away; their vaulting **ambition** overleaped itself, however, and they miserably failed (B. H. Roberts, *The Life of John Taylor*, 348).

But the man recognized by most observers as the most **ambitious** in the early Church was John C. Bennett. His original motives for joining the Church are suspect, but they appear to have been piqued by its dynamic achievements and claims of authority. He perceived opportunities to gain from his considerable talents and influence.

> Dr. John C. Bennett was described as "a man of enterprise, extensive acquirements, and of independent mind, one calculated to be of great benefit to the Church. . . ." When he contemplated joining his fortunes with the Church at Commerce, he held the position of quartermaster-general in the militia of the State

of Illinois, a position he did not wish to resign. . . . He was also a physician with an extensive practice. . . . [Bennett proclaimed] "your people shall have the benefit of my speaking power, and my untiring energies in behalf of the good and holy faith."

The egotism of the man plainly appears in these expressions, and manifests a spirit that is altogether at variance with the humility required by the Gospel, and doubtless that self-importance laid the foundation of his subsequent fall (B. H. Roberts, *Comprehensive History of the Church*, 2:73).

Not long after Bennett joined the Church in September 1840, he was elected Mayor of Nauvoo and then appointed a Major-General in the Nauvoo Legion and Chancellor of the University of Nauvoo. The following year he was called to be a Counselor to the Prophet. All of these high positions were very satisfying to his huge ego and undoubtedly contributed to a feeling of superiority. In any event, he soon after became involved with several women, several of whom succumbed to his lustful desires, justified by his claims that sexual intercourse was countenanced by the Prophet, if it was kept secret. When confronted by the Prophet, he gave a tearful confession; however, he soon returned to his lustful practices.

At first glance it may be difficult to comprehend how a character like John C. Bennett could find favor and place with the Church of Christ. There is a strong temptation, when the whole truth about this man is known, to regard him as an adventurer and a wicked man from the beginning. But those who had, perhaps, the best opportunity to know him held that his motives for coming to Nauvoo were honest, that his intentions in life at that time were honorable, but that he fell into transgression and would not repent. Such were the views of John Taylor, who was closely associated with Bennett in affairs at Nauvoo, and the Lord in the revelation given on the 19th of January, 1841, accepts of him and speaks approvingly of Bennett's love for the work: "And for his love he shall be great. . . . I have seen the work which he hath done, which I accept, if he continue, and will crown him with blessings and great glory" (Joseph Smith, *History of the Church*, 5:xvii).

Unfortunately, the feelings of some members in the Church are that one should have a long list of callings on their personal resume. Those who have such a list are held in respect and reverence. If we do not have such a list, we may feel that we have failed in our stewardship. On the other hand, a righteous desire to serve is commendable. In 1 Timothy 3:1, the Apostle Paul counsels: "This is a true saying, If a man desire the office of a bishop, he desireth a good work."

Elder Alexander Morrison has recognized the potential dangers in the adulation that can occur between Church leaders and members:

> How seductive the lure of power and the prestige that goes with it can be! The acclaim of the people, the virtual adulation in which leaders are held by many members, the hanging-on-every-word attention leaders receive—all are powerful intoxicants, easily capable of corrupting the unwary shepherd. Leaders should, of course, be grateful for the love and support of the Saints. But they must discount personal praise directed at them, recognizing that whatever fraction is deserved rightfully belongs to the Good Shepherd and the Father. We can take little credit if we utilize well gifts and talents that have been bestowed upon us. The credit belongs to the Giver of Gifts, not the receiver. When dealing with the praise of men, perhaps it would be wise to adopt something of the attitude of the Duke of Wellington. Asked if he were pleased to have been mobbed by the ecstatic population of Brussels on his return from Waterloo, (Wellington) rejoined, "Not in the least; if I had failed, they would have shot me" (Alexander Morrison, *Feed My Sheep*, 169).

George Q. Cannon counseled the following regarding church positions:

> The only principle upon which position should be sought and held by the servants of God is that they might thereby be more useful—that the field of their usefulness might be enlarged. No man should seek to hold a position to gratify a vain **ambition** to excel. And whatever the position that may be assigned him, he should therewith be content. If an Elder's happiness be affected by the prominence or obscurity of his station, it is an evidence that he is dependent upon something beside the Spirit of God for happiness; if he be appointed to labor in a humble position by those who have the authority and he strives to fill that appointment honorably, he will be happy—his happiness will be perfect; his joy will be full; should his station be ever so exalted, he could be no more than this (George Q. Cannon, *Gospel Truths*, 181).

The Melchizedek Priesthood was taught that "loyalty requires us to put away selfishness, greed, **ambition** and all of the baser qualities of the human mind. You cannot be loyal unless you are willing to surrender. . . . [A person's] own preferences and desires must be put away, and he must see only the great purpose which lies ahead" (*Immortality and Eternal Life*, Melchizedek Priesthood Course of Study, 1968–69, 163).

President Cannon also gives a positive tilt to **ambition**, when we couch it in a desire to become like our Heavenly Father:

> God controls the earth and the inhabitants thereof. . . . He will give us an equal interest in all this power and authority. What is more desirable to man, generally speaking, than to wield power? Mankind aim for it. To what lengths will **ambitious** men go to wield power, to sit upon thrones and to wield a sceptre of authority. History tells us that men have been willing to wade through seas of blood to gratify this **ambition.**

63

Now, this **ambition** can be gratified righteously by keeping the commandments of God, and a righteous man will exercise righteous authority. That is the object God had in view in sending us here. Through faithfully keeping His commandments we may attain exaltation and for the exaltation of other human beings.

It is God's design to make us priests and kings, not to have an empty title, not to sit upon thrones without power but to actually and really be priests and kings. The promise is that all things that He hath shall be given unto us. We will be His heirs; we will be (if I may use the term without irreverence) co-partners with Him in all this power and authority (George Q. Cannon, *Gospel Truths*, 88).

To attain the blessings suggested by President Cannon, and to avoid the **ambition** that leads to apostasy, we can learn and live the counsel the Lord gave to the Prophet Joseph in the depths of his despair in the Liberty jail, and to each of us:

Behold, many are called, but few are chosen. And why are they not chosen?

Because their hearts are set so much upon the things of this world, and aspire to the honors of men, that they do not learn this one lesson—

That the rights of the priesthood are inseparably connected with the powers of heaven, and that the powers of heaven cannot be controlled nor handled only upon the principles of righteousness.

That they may be conferred upon us, it is true; but when we undertake to cover our sins, or to gratify our pride, our vain **ambition**, or to exercise control or dominion or compulsion upon the souls of the children of men, in any degree of unrighteousness, behold, the heavens withdraw themselves; the Spirit of the Lord is grieved; and when it is withdrawn, Amen to the priesthood or the authority of that man.

64

Behold, ere he is aware, he is left unto himself, to kick against the pricks, to persecute the saints, and to fight against God.

We have learned by sad experience that it is the nature and disposition of almost all men, as soon as they get a little authority, as they suppose, they will immediately begin to exercise unrighteous dominion.

Hence many are called, but few are chosen.

No power or influence can or ought to be maintained by virtue of the priesthood, only by persuasion, by long-suffering, by gentleness and meekness, and by love unfeigned.

By kindness, and pure knowledge, which shall greatly enlarge the soul without hypocrisy, and without guile.

Reproving betimes with sharpness, when moved upon by the Holy Ghost; and then showing forth afterwards an increase of love toward him whom thou hast reproved, lest he esteem thee to be his enemy.

That he may know that thy faithfulness is stronger than the cords of death.

Let thy bowels also be full of charity towards all men, and to the household of faith, and let virtue garnish your thoughts unceasingly; then shall thy confidence wax strong in the presence of God; and the doctrine of the priesthood shall distil upon thy soul as the dews from heaven

The Holy Ghost shall be thy constant companion, and thy scepter an unchanging scepter of righteousness and truth; and thy dominion shall be an everlasting dominion, and without compulsory means it shall flow unto thee forever and ever (D&C 121:34–46).

Thus, in this great revelation, we receive God's counsel:

- Rights come through righteousness.
- Power comes from virtuous behavior.

- Love and charity confirm our true self.
- Then, we are blessed with God's approval, the Holy Spirit, and eternal glory.

DON'T SEEK THE SPIRIT

After the death of the Prophet Joseph Smith, Brigham Young had a dream in which Joseph appeared to him with the following advice: "Tell the brethren if they will follow the **spirit of the Lord** they will go right. Be sure to tell the people to keep the **Spirit**" (Brigham Young, *Manuscript History of Brigham Young 1846–1847*, 529).

Unfortunately, some converts who joined the Church in the early days were baptized, and left the Church soon after. Some were impressed with the missionaries and believed their testimonies. Others observed or experienced miracles, and were convinced of the efficacy of the restored church. Still others were touched by the **spirit** with a conviction of the message of the Gospel. The testimonies of these converts were like the seed that was sown in stony places, "where they had not much earth: and forthwith they sprung up, because they had no deepness of earth: And when the sun was up, they were scorched; and because they had no root, they withered away" (Matt. 13:5–6).

Brigham Young expressed great concern that men and women joined the Church but **did not seek the spirit** that would help them to progress in their becoming Saints. They failed to understand that to have the companionship of the **Holy Ghost** one must do all of those things that ensure it's **being with us.** At minimum, we must repent, pray for it, and obey the commandments and our covenants. Is it possible that one would not want to have the blessings of the **Spirit**? Or, coming from a gentile world, that one would not know that he needs or should have the **Spirit**?

The **"gifts of the Spirit"** was a distinguishing feature of the restored Gospel that attracted many of the early converts—the Cambellites in Kirtland, the independent sect led by John Taylor in Canada, and the independent groups in England proselyted by Heber C. Kimball and Wilford Woodruff. They had read in the Bible about the various **gifts of the Spirit**, and pondered and prayed that these **gifts** could be obtained in their day.

The cares of the world have a strong pull on those who have just entered the waters of baptism. They have just left a life that has filled their thoughts and activity with traditions, friends and family, work and play, habits, and numerous other things that were familiar to them. Unless the new environment of the Church and its members are responsive and prompt, the convert may revert to his or her former ways. It is not sufficient that the convert receive the **gift of the Spirit** at baptism, unless he or she understands that its influence will lead them on to greater understanding and the blessings of the restored Gospel. Thus, how vital are fellowshipping and participation in the programs of the Church.

President Joseph Fielding Smith observed that some converts join because the gospel is logical and consistent, but they never exert themselves to get the **Spirit of the Lord**. Others have ulterior motives for joining and consequently never receive the light.

James Covill was given a great promise by the Lord, if he would be baptized and preach the fullness of the gospel (D&C 39). He was an experienced minister of the gospel, whose talent and experience would have contributed much to the missionary effort of the new Church. But before he obtained a spiritual confirmation, so that he could keep his covenant, "Satan tempted him, and the fear of persecution and the cares of the world caused him to reject the word" (D&C 40:2).

About a month after Covill's rejection, Leman Copley was baptized. He was honest-hearted but he still retained some of the ideas of the Shaker faith. He was assigned to go with Sidney Rigdon and Parley P. Pratt to visit the Shaker society, where they were rebuffed. Then he contracted to allow the Colesville Saints to settle on his large farm under the law of stewardship. When he learned that stewardship meant consecrating his property to the Church, he reneged on his commitment to the Colesville group, who were forced to move on to Missouri. It seems that Leman never gained a full testimony of the true gospel, which comes only through the aid of the **Spirit**. He was so preoccupied with temporal matters, alienating the **Spirit** and failing to join in communion with the Saints.

The scriptures provide plenteous counsel regarding the need for us to have the **Spirit**, as well as the consequences if we fail to seek its direction. Through the Prophet Alma the Lord declared:

> The spirits of the wicked, yea, who are evil—for behold, they have no part nor portion of the **Spirit** of the Lord; for behold, they chose evil works rather than good; therefore the **spirit** of the devil did enter into them, and take possession of their house—and these shall be cast out into outer darkness; there shall be weeping, and wailing, and gnashing of teeth, and this because of their own iniquity, being led captive by the will of the devil (Alma 40:13).

Elder Bruce R. McConkie counseled a BYU audience that:

> We should seek to get in tune with the **Holy Spirit** and to gain a witness, not solely of the truth and divinity of the work in which we are engaged but also

of the doctrines that are taught by those who preach to us. We come into these congregations, and sometimes a speaker brings a jug of living water that has in it many gallons. And he pours it out on the congregation, all that the members have brought is a single cup and so that's all they take away. Or maybe they have their hands over the cups, and they don't get anything to speak of.

On other occasions we have meetings where the speaker comes and all he brings is a little cup of eternal truth, and the members of the congregation come with a large jug, and all they get in their jugs is the little dribble that came from a man who should have known better and who should have prepared himself and talked from the revelations and spoken by the power of the **Spirit** (Bruce R. McConkie in a BYU Address, "The Seven Deadly Heresies," June 1, 1980).

Elder Carlos Asay described another viewpoint regarding how we are prepared to receive **inspiration** in church meetings:

We sometimes use the expressions "out of tune" or "in tune" in reference to people and worship services. The first expression describes those who drag the world into sacred settings and attempt to pay their devotions to God with half of their mind in Babylon and the other half in Zion. Since they are "double-minded" men and women, their actions are unstable and their words are contaminated. On the other hand, those who are "in tune" come before the Lord at home or at church with humble spirits and eyes upward. They have blocked out the lesser things of the world and are ready to receive instructions from on high (Carlos Asay, *Family Pecan Trees*, 204).

Apostle Amasa Lyman presents one of the most interesting cases of not listening to the **spirit**. In October 1857 he spoke in the Salt Lake Tabernacle, after having been a member for 25 years, and one of the great missionaries of this dispensation. He spoke about the need and blessing of the **Holy Spirit**:

> Apostates are found as we pass through the country, and they will say, "I knew the work to be true twenty years ago; I knew that it was then." You did not know the Gospel; you did not understand it; you might have known or felt conscious that what some man told you was true. But is the **spirit** of the Gospel to that man that comprehends it? It is that which comprehends all truth and all good; and there is no truth, neither is there any good outside it; and there is, consequently, no chance for the individual that views the Gospel of Jesus Christ in this **light** . . . that cause them to apostatize.
>
> Does a man get away from the truth by apostasy? . . . When he opens his eyes, there is the truth; God is there, his influences are there, his **Spirit** is there. . . . You want to live so that your minds will be filled with his **Spirit** . . . do that which brings peace—that which produces the **spirit** of peace and of heaven.
>
> And if you open a door that this **Spirit** will take up his abode with you, then that fountain will be opened up will be plenteous in its supplies; it will become so to you because you welcome the **Holy Spirit** there, and you study to cultivate within you such a feeling that the **spirit** will love to tarry with you day by day; and its book of instructions will be opened to you, so that each succeeding day will give you an increase of knowledge, and you will find yourselves able to comprehend one degree of light and knowledge after another, until your whole soul will be swallowed up in your love for the truth; your affections will be bound up in the truth, for which you will be willing to sacrifice all (Amasa Lyman, *Journal of Discourses*, 5:307–10) (1857).

Five years later, Brother Lyman was Mission President in London. In Dundee, Scotland, he preached that Jesus was just a "holy man" and that the atonement was not needed. After confessing his error and asking for forgiveness, he continued to serve until 1867, when he reneged on his promise and was accused of teaching again this false doctrine. After being disfellowshipped, he joined the "New Movement", an apostate group that espoused spiritualism. He was listening to the wrong "spirit," which led to his excommunication in 1870.

Would that Elder Lyman had followed the word of the Lord that was given to Joseph Smith and Sidney Rigdon at the conclusion of the great revelation on the three degrees of glory:

> But great and marvelous are the works of the Lord, and the mysteries of his kingdom which he showed unto us, which surpass all understanding in glory, and in might, and in dominion;
>
> Which he commanded us we should not write while we were yet in the **Spirit,** and are not lawful for man to utter;
>
> Neither is man capable to make them known, for they are only to be seen and understood by the power of the **Holy Spirit**, which God bestows on those who love him, and purify themselves before him. . . .
>
> That through the power and manifestation of the **spirit**, while in the flesh, they may be able to bear his presence in the world of glory. (D&C 76:114–16, 118)

Parley P. Pratt, who enjoyed many blessings of the **Holy Spirit** wrote that: "The **gift of the Holy Ghost** . . . inspires, develops, cultivates, and matures all the fine-toned affections of our nature. It inspires virtue, kindness, goodness, tenderness, gentleness, and charity" (Parley P. Pratt, *Key to the Science of Theology*, 101).

John the Beloved explained that "the **Comforter** . . . shall teach you all things" (John 14:26).

President Marion G. Romney told students at Brigham Young University in 1979:

If you want to obtain and keep the guidance of the **Spirit**, you can do so by following this simple four-point program:

> "One, pray. Pray diligently. . . . Learn to talk to the Lord; call upon his name in great faith and confidence.
>
> Second, study and learn the gospel.
>
> Third, live righteously; repent of your sins by confessing them and forsaking them. Then conform to the teachings of the gospel.
>
> Fourth, give service in the Church" (Marion G. Romney, *The Ensign*, January 1980, 5).

President Harold B. Lee was one who understood well the need that we have for the **Holy Spirit**.

> The new First Presidency held a news conference in the administration building with many members of the press in attendance. One reporter asked President Lee if he would mind explaining what his goals were. He asked: "What do you expect to accomplish during your administration as president of the Church?"
>
> President Lee answered in his most characteristic way, substantially as follows: "Well," he said, "I can only answer that question in the words of a great prophet when he was given an assignment by the Lord to secure an ancient record. He said: 'And I was led by the **Spirit**, not knowing beforehand the things which I should do'" (Hartman Rector Jr., *The Ensign*, January 1974, 105).

If we would have the **spirit**, we can well follow President Romney's advice to **pray, study, repent, live righteously,** and **serve faithfully.**

FEAR OF PERSECUTION

In the early days of the restoration of the gospel and the priesthood, **persecution** was centered on Joseph Smith in Harmony, Pennsylvania and Palmyra, New York. Joseph was hounded by ruffians seeking the gold plates. At Harmony and Colesville vexatious law suits were repeatedly brought against the young Prophet, without conviction.

When the Church moved to Kirtland, Ohio, persecution expanded to other leaders of the Church and to the missionaries. In addition to various law suits, Joseph and Sidney Rigdon were tarred and feathered at Hiram. Following the failure of the Kirtland Safety Society Anti-Banking Company in 1837, the dissidents and apostates under the leadership of Warren Parrish attempted to take over the Church and oust Joseph, while he was away on missionary duties. Under threat of injury and death from the Parrish faction, Joseph and other leaders escaped to Far West, Missouri, in December 1837.

In the meantime, in Jackson County, Missouri, after an initial period of calm, violence touched all of the Saints who suffered from looting, beatings and destruction of their homes. They were driven across the Missouri River and north to further and more intensive violence in Clay and Caldwell Counties. This escalating violence brought on the massacre at Haun's Mill, the battle at Crooked River and the betrayal of the Prophet and other Church leaders at Far West.

Apostates testified against those leaders and precipitated the issuance of the Extermination Order by Governor

Lilburn W. Boggs. These dire circumstances caused many Saints to abandon their religion for **fear** of suffering death, injury, spoilation of their property or violation of their virtue.

At Nauvoo in the early 1840s there was a season of peace and prosperity. Then a coterie of apostates from among Church leaders, plus a lingering conspiracy emanating from Missouri, agitated the riffraff in neighboring counties to mob violence. Joseph and Hyrum Smith were murdered, and the Saints were driven from their beautiful Nauvoo into the uncharted wilds to the west. Perhaps thousands of the Saints failed to go west with Brigham Young and the Twelve, preferring to renounce their faith, religion and practices rather than endure **persecution,** hardship and the unknown terrors, real or imagined, of the lands beyond the frontier.

While the Saints felt much more secure in their homes in the mountains, they were hounded by seemingly endless federal territorial appointees, who were determined to whip the Saints into line. Laws were passed, primarily against the practice of polygamy, that increasingly proscribed the Church and its members. Finally the United States Government moved to seize Church assets and properties, stopped only at the last moment by the declaration by President Wilford Woodruff of the Manifesto, that announced the cessation of plural marriages. Once more, many members chose to renounce their allegiance for a variety of reasons, only one of which was polygamy.

Persecution may come in many forms; however, one of the most fearful is one's anticipation of future persecution, which not infrequently exceeds reality. William Shakespeare describes this condition well in the words of Hamlet:

> And makes us rather bear those ills we have,
> than to fly to others that we know not of?
>
> Thus conscience does make cowards of us all. . . .
> (*Hamlet*, act 3, scene 1)

In Fayette, New York, James Covill had covenanted that he would obey any command that the Lord would give to him through Joseph the Prophet. A wonderful blessing was promised James in a revelation to the Prophet in D&C 39 on January 5, 1831. Before the end of that month Joseph Smith received a short revelation, wherein the Lord said:

> "And he [James Covill] received the word with gladness, but straightway Satan tempted him; and the **fear of persecution** and the cares of the world caused him to reject the word. Wherefore he broke my covenant. . . ." (D&C 40:2, 3).

At the critical moment when James Covill might have pursued the path leading to eternal life, the evil one attacked and led him away from the very goal he had desired to achieve.

James Covill's experience can be seen as being representative of what happens to many people. Everyone faces critical moments of making decisions, setting goals, and establishing commitments pertaining to future behavior. It is at these critical times that Lucifer enters into the battle to persuade us against pursuing courses of righteousness. He knows we are likely to become spiritually stronger as time goes by as we honor and keep our commitments with the Lord. Consequently, he seems determined to "straightway" tempt us. Satan employs many methods as deflectors from our true course.

It was very difficult for James Covill to leave friends, associations, professional security, etc., that had long provided him with mortal comforts. When he took time to consider the realities and implications of his decision to forsake it all and enter the Church of the Savior, he weakened. Satan's influence overcame him, he broke his covenant with the Lord, and forsook his opportunity to receive and share the fullness of the gospel of Jesus Christ (L. G. Otten and C. M. Caldwell, *Sacred Truths of the Doctrine and Covenants*, 189–90).

The *Times and Seasons* described the ominous condition, when the Missouri militia was advancing on Far West in late October 1838:

> They saw that it was impossible to conquer a people who were fighting for their homes, and their wives and children, unless they could come against them with some show of authority, for it was a well known fact, that the Mormons never resisted authority, however abused; therefore their next exertion was to spread lies and falsehoods of the most alarming character; such as the Mormons were in a state of rebellion against the Government, and that they were about to burn Richmond, etc. This flame was greatly assisted by several in high authority who deserted from the church, and fell away to the robbers because of **fear**, and also for the sake of power and gain. These deserters became far more false, hardened and bloodthirsty, than those who had never known the way of righteousness, insomuch that they were filled with all manner of lying and murders, and plundering (*Times and Seasons*, 1:114).

There is little doubt that Colonel George Hinkle was **fearful** for his safety in his betrayal of Church leaders to General Lucas and the Missouri militia on October 31, 1838, at Far West. In the subsequent treason trial of Joseph Smith and fifty-five others at Richmond, apostates John Corrill, Sampson Avard, Thomas B. Marsh, W. W. Phelps and others testified that Joseph, Hyrum and Sidney were the founders and leaders of the *Danite Band* dedicated to hunting down and killing local citizens, including apostates. Some have said that their actions were likely the product of both **fear of persecution** and for personal gain. It was during these dangerous times that the Whitmer family, and son-in-law Oliver Cowdery, withdrew their support from the Church, and were either excommunicated or left the Church. **Fear** of physical harm was definitely a factor in Oliver's defection, and likely also with his in-laws.

Christian Whitmer, died in 1835 from the abuse of mobs in Missouri. On one occasion, he faced a mob when they, with the muzzle of a gun in his face, threatened to kill him if he did not tell them where they could find his brethren who had escaped. Many other Saints endured similar perilous situations, including the martyrdom of Apostle David Patten and two others at the Battle of Crooked River.

Oftentimes the **fear of persecution** was endured vicariously, when wives would wait anxiously with their children for news of their imprisoned mates. Certainly Emma Smith could be identified as one who would have frequently suffered silently for word of the fate of her Prophet husband. Emma's household duties were a grave responsibility which demanded most of her attention. Scarcely a day passed but some dear friend or curious stranger called at their home and was invited to remain for dinner or even spend a few days with them. They had placed three children in the silent tomb. The persecution in Missouri filled her with **fear** and **apprehension** and robbed her of the time she could have spent in selecting hymns for the Church.

There was a reverse pitch given to **fear of persecution** in the perilous days just before and after the martyrdom of Joseph and Hyrum Smith in 1844. William Law and John C. Bennett, among others, complained that they feared reprisal from the Danites in Nauvoo, whom they thought were instructed to injure and even kill them. These claims had been circulated by apostates and dissidents as far back as the expulsion of the Saints from Missouri, and would persist for decades afterward even in the valleys of Utah.

An article in the *Improvement Era* of 1905 deals with this **reverse fear**:

> We hear much of men not daring to apostatize from the Church, because they **fear** for their lives, property and interests! Who among the Saints has ever injured an apostate? On the contrary, he brings

his own punishment upon himself, the Saints do him no harm. Any man who says he is hampered by the Saints because he has turned away from the gospel, does not tell the truth. You know, the people, young and old, know that I am telling the truth. If any persecution is reported among this people, let it be known, and the bishops of those who persecute will be asked to have them taught their duty, which is to fear the Lord and love all men. I would have the people taught that if an enemy in our midst has sickness, let him be visited; if he is naked, clothe him; if there is a stranger in our midst, comfort him. It has always been a doctrine of the Church, her leaders, and her people, as well as their practice, to love all men and let judgment rest with the Lord; to do good to all men, to bless and not to curse. The practice and the doctrine are in force today as ever. (Improvement Era, February, 1905. "The Truth Remains." Joseph F. Smith).

President George Q. Cannon counseled the Saints in the October 1900 General Conference regarding **persecution**:

God has said: "And whoso layeth down his life in my cause, for my name's sake, shall find it again, even life eternal. Therefore, be **not afraid** of your enemies, for I have decreed in my heart, saith the Lord, that I will prove you in all things. whether you will abide in my covenant, even unto death, that you may be found worthy" (D&C 98:13–14).

And again He says: "And all they who **suffer persecution** for my name, and endure in faith, though they are called to lay down their lives for my sake yet shall they partake of all this glory. Wherefor, fear not even unto death; for in this world your joy is not full, but in me your joy is full" (D&C 101:35–36).

But while we should not shrink from complying with every requirement, we ought to **avoid persecution** and death by every means in our power that would be honorable and consistent with our duties and obligations. But in preaching this Gospel to the nations of the earth we ought not to be afraid of our liberty or our lives. (George Q. Cannon, *Gospel Truths*, 153)

President Brigham Young understood full well the thinking of the Saints, faithful and otherwise, to which he commented as follows at April General Conference in April 1855:

> I say to the Latter-day Saints, who are coming here by thousands and thousands, and who are coming into the Church by tens of thousands, begin to think, especially some of you first Elders, and ask yourselves how many you can bring to mind of those who are now in good faith in the Church, in proportion to the number that you have known to have come into it, and you will find that there are only a *very few.*
>
> If you should hunt up many of these who have been baptized for some time, but have not yet gathered, and ask them . . . why don't you gather with the Saints? . . . "If I go there I shall be **persecuted**, but if I live here I shall have peace with my neighbors, so long as I let religious matters alone, and here I can live **without persecution**." What makes them have that **fear** of trials and **persecution**? It is because of their tabernacles. The spirit is not afraid. If it was free of the encumbrances of the tabernacle, no such **fear** would be manifested; and while we are in the flesh the Gospel is calculated to deliver those who live by its principles from all those **fears.**
>
> I recollect many times when brother Joseph, reflecting upon how many would come into the Kingdom of God and go out again, would say, "Brethren, I have not apostatized yet, and don't feel like doing so." Many of you, no doubt, can call to mind his words. Joseph had to pray all the time, exercise faith, live his religion, and magnify his calling, to obtain the manifestations of the Lord, and to keep him steadfast in the faith.
>
> Do you not know others who had manifestations almost equal to those Joseph had, but who have gone by the board? Martin Harris declared, before God and

81

angels, that he had seen angels. Did he apostatize? Yes, though he says that the Book of Mormon is true. Oliver Cowdery also left the Church, though he never denied the Book of Mormon, not even in the wickedest days he ever saw, and came back into the Church before he died. . . . After he had left the Church he still believed "Mormonism," and so it is with hundreds and thousands of others, and yet they do not live it (Brigham Young, *Journal of Discourses*, 2:257). [1855]

In our time, there is still persecution of Latter-day Saints in many foreign lands, where the Church is just putting down roots. There will be trials and **persecution** for the faithful, and there will be defections unless the new converts are embraced in the arms of brotherhood. Even then, the draw of family and old friends and habits will exert strong temptations to lure them away.

A living Authority, Elder Neal A. Maxwell, helps us recognize the challenge that faces us:

Just how effectively the devil can mount a two-front war against us is seen in the words of the Lord wherein he speaks of "the **fear of persecution** and the cares of the world." (D&C 40:2) If our appetites can be directed in such a way that we are caught up in the cares of the world, and if we are then also **afraid of persecution** because of doing what is right, we have been acted upon and are doubly deterred from discipleship. Some who might not **fear persecution** by itself do not choose to cope with the double load of **persecution** plus the cares of the world. Some for whom the cares of the world would not be sufficient to draw them away finally yield because of the **fear of persecution.**

Another dimension of this strain of similarities running through the scriptures can be seen in those scriptures that pertain to the weaknesses we have in life and how, though some are given to us of God to keep us humble, such defects can actually be a strength to us. The Lord assures us that "my grace is sufficient for all men that humble themselves before me" (Ether 12:26–27) (Neal A. Maxwell, *Things As They Really Are*, 90).

We recognize that with greater knowledge and blessings, there is a demand for greater accountability. Not only do we have four books of scriptures, and continuing revelation and guidance from "prophets, seers and revelators," but at baptism we receive the gift of the Holy Ghost to guide us personally. As we seek and qualify for the Spirit, we may then receive an understanding of the fullness of the mysteries of God. Consequently, we thus are obligated to behave and serve in a superior way, growing from grace to grace.

This concept of greater accountability has been understood by the faithful from Palmyra to our day. But thousands of converts never gained that vision, but were confused and frightened by the cares of the world and the **fear of persecution**. Apostle George Q. Cannon taught this concept to the Saints in July 1872:

> The Latter-day Saints, I hold, will be held to stricter accountability than any other people on the face of the earth. Men wonder why we have suffered and been **persecuted** so much in the past. I think it was partly because of our hardness of heart. Not that the men who **persecuted** us were justified in so doing. They were tested and tried, the Lord left them their agency and they brought themselves under condemnation because of their conduct. But we never had anything descend upon us as a **persecution** or scourge that has not been intended for our good; and we are held to a stricter accountability than any other people because we have the Gospel taught unto us.
>
> The thousands who live throughout these valleys testify that they have received the Holy Ghost; they testify that they received it in the lands where they embraced the Gospel; they say that this love which they have for one another, and the disposition they have to dwell together in peace and unity are the fruits of this Holy Spirit that they have received.

When a people reach this condition they are held to stricter accountability than they are who have not this knowledge. On this account we must walk circumspectly, with the fear of God before our eyes. We must be a pure people or we will be scourged; we must be a holy people, or God's anger will be kindled against us. We must not be guilty of dishonesty or take advantage one of another; we must not bear false witness; we must not neglect our duties one to another or towards God, for we can not do these things with impunity, for God's anger will be kindled against us; and in proportion to the light which men have will they be judged, and God will reward them according to the deeds done in the body . . . and the man who has heard the sound of the everlasting Gospel and the testimony of the servants of God is held to stricter accountability than he who has never heard them (George Q. Cannon, *Journal of Discourses*, 15:119). [1872]

In many ways, Mormons today are greatly respected around the world. In some respects, this is a wonderful turnaround, paving the way for greater access to seekers of righteousness by our missionaries. But it may also lead us to be soft and tolerant to the ways of the world.

As several Church leaders who had survived the trials of Missouri and Nauvoo have commented, the faith and commitment that was required by the faithful in those sore days made them a Zion-like people. They sacrificed for one another, and for the Lord's work.

We have been warned in the scriptures that frightful times will come in the latter days, prior to the second coming of our Lord. In preparation for those times to come, we must turn to the **warnings** and the **promises** of the Lord through the prophets, ancient and modern. They tell what is expected of us. Furthermore, we have living prophets who are enlightened by the Holy Spirit, and by long experience, to prepare us for the trials and persecution to come.

Our challenge is to hear, believe, and obey in wisdom and faith. **"If ye are prepared, ye shall not fear"** (D&C 38:30).

PROSPERITY AND RICHES

One of the abiding impressions of those who have read the Book of Mormon is the repeated cycle of **prosperity and riches** that led to pride, wickedness and decline to repentance to **prosperity and riches** again. One wonders why the Nephites did not learn from the experiences of their forefathers to avoid the bondage and misery that they repeatedly endured.

The Lord through his prophets has warned his chosen children again and again of the consequences of hewing to their **riches** and neglecting the poor and their duties. The Savior taught his disciples on several occasions that they were to focus their time and energies on "treasures . . . where moth and rust doth not corrupt" (Matt. 6:20).

A certain ruler asked Jesus what he should do to inherit eternal life. The commandments that Jesus mentioned the ruler had kept from his youth. Then Jesus told him:

> Yet lackest thou one thing: sell all that thou hast, and distribute unto the poor, and thou shalt have treasure in heaven; and come follow me.
>
> And when he heard this, he was very sorrowful: for he was **very rich**.
>
> And when Jesus saw that he was very sorrowful, he said, How hardly shall they that have **riches** enter into the kingdom of God (Luke 18:22–24)!

Of this situation, Elder Milton R. Hunter observed,

> And why will it be so difficult for a **rich man** to enter into the kingdom of heaven? Because ofttimes **riches**

canker the souls of men and make it impossible for them to put first things first and love the Lord their God with all of their hearts, might, mind and strength. Jesus described aptly such people in his parable of the sower. To quote: "He also that receiveth seed among the thorns is he that heareth the word, and the care of this world, and the deceitfulness of **riches,** choke the word, and he becometh unfruitful" (Milton R. Hunter, *Will a Man Rob God?* 139).

From the earliest times the Lord has reminded man of his responsibility to care for the poor and the needy. Jesus taught this concept in the parable of Lazarus and the **Rich Man,** including the consequences of not remembering and serving those in need. Jesus told the following story:

There was a certain **rich man**, which was clothed in purple and fine linen, and fared sumptuously every day:

And there was a certain beggar named Lazarus, which was laid at his gate, full of sores,

And desiring to be fed with the crumbs which fell from the rich man's table: moreover the dogs came and licked his sores.

And it came to pass, that the beggar died, and was carried by the angels into Abraham's bosom: the **rich man** also died, and was buried;

And in hell he lift up his eyes, being in torments, and seeth Abraham afar off, and Lazarus in his bosom.

And he cried and said, Father Abraham, have mercy on me, and send Lazarus, that he may dip the tip of his finger in water, and cool my tongue; for I am tormented in this flame.

But Abraham said, Son, remember that thou in thy lifetime receivest thy **good things**, and likewise Lazarus evil things: but now he is comforted, and thou art tormented (Luke 16:19–25).

Jesus observed, "That a **rich man** shall hardly enter into the kingdom of heaven. . . . It is easier for a camel to go through the eye of a needle, than for a **rich man** to enter into the kingdom of God."

Apostle James E. Talmage gave an interesting interpretation of this scripture in Matthew 19:24–6:

> Some interpreters insist that a rope, not a camel, was mentioned by Jesus, and these base their contention on the fact that the Greek word *kamelos* (camel) differs in but a single letter from *kamilos* (rope), and that the alleged error of substituting "camel" for "rope" in the scriptural text is chargeable to the early copyists. Farrar (p. 476) rejects this possible interpretation on the ground that proverbs involving comparisons of a kind with that of a camel passing through the eye of a needle are common in the Talmud.
>
> It has been asserted that the term "needle's eye" was applied to a small door or wicket set in or alongside the great gates in the walls of cities; and the assumption has been raised that Jesus had such a wicket in mind when He spoke of the seeming impossibility of a camel passing through a needle's eye. It would be possible though very difficult for a camel to squeeze its way through the little gate, and it could in no wise do so except when relieved of its load and stripped of all its harness. If this conception be correct, we may find additional similitude between the fact that the camel must first be unloaded and stripped, however costly its burden or **rich** its accoutrement, and the necessity of the **rich** young ruler, and so of any man, divesting himself of the burden and trappings of wealth, if he would enter by the narrow way that leadeth into the kingdom (James E. Talmage, *Jesus the Christ*, 450).

In the Book of Mormon King Benjamin's great farewell sermon to his beloved people contains the following advice:

> For the sake of retaining a remission of your sins from day to day, that ye may walk guiltless before God—I would that ye should impart of your **substance** to the poor, every man according to that which he

hath, such as feeding the hungry, clothing the naked, visiting the sick and administering to their relief, both spiritually and temporally, according to their wants (Mosiah 4:26).

The Apostle Paul gave similar counsel to Timothy:

Charge them that are **rich** in this world, that they be not highminded, nor trust in uncertain **riches**, but in the living God, who giveth us **richly** all things to enjoy; that they do good, that they be **rich** in good works, ready to distribute, willing to communicate; laying up in store for themselves a good foundation against the time to come, that they may lay hold on eternal life (1 Tim. 6:17–19).

Those who are **rich** usually reward themselves with luxuriant homes, cars, appliances, clothing and activities. Not surprisingly, they associate with others who enjoy similar adornments and tastes. Having invested in costly and plentiful possessions, the **rich** spend much time and thought on their upkeep and maintenance. In our day of enjoying possessions now, and paying for them in the future, the **rich** may have need of making sizeable installments that will also occupy their attention. In this condition requiring constant concern for maintaining a demanding life style, the **rich** can easily be distracted from church duties and the concerns or needs of others.

President Spencer W. Kimball observed that

the possession of **riches** does not necessarily constitute sin. But sin may arise in the acquisition and use of **wealth.** In the Book of Mormon, each time the people became righteous, they **prospered.** Then followed the transition from **prosperity** to **wealth, wealth** to the love of **wealth,** then to the love of ease and luxury. They moved then into spiritual inactivity, then to gross sin and wickedness, then on to near destruction by their enemies. This caused them to repent, which brought back righteousness, then **prosperity,** and the cycle had begun all over again (Spencer W. Kimball, *Miracle of Forgiveness*, 47).

Apostle George Q. Cannon offers a more promising prospect that all of us can hope and strive for:

> The Scriptures say that a **rich** man would hardly enter the kingdom of heaven, but it does not mean that riches will condemn a man, not at all. God is pleased to see us acquire **riches,** for he intends ultimately to give to us the whole earth as an eternal inheritance, but it is the love of **riches** that kills. A great gulf separates those who enter the house of the Lord and take wives, and those who do not thus marry (i.e., do not choose to qualify)—a tremendous gulf, but to the unspiritual eye no difference is apparent (George Q. Cannon, *Gospel Doctrine*, 97).

In commenting on the behavior of apostates Brigham Young reminded the Saints in 1853:

> This people commenced with nothing. Joseph Smith, the honored instrument in the hands of God to lay the foundation of this work, commenced with nothing; he had neither the wisdom nor the **riches** of this world. And it is proven to our satisfaction, that when **rich** men have come into this Church, the Lord has been determined to take their **riches** from them and make them poor; that all His Saints may learn to obtain that which they possess by faith.
>
> How many times has he made us poor? Thousands of dollars' worth of property in houses and lands, which the Lord gave me, are now in the East, in the hands of our enemies. I never said they were mine, they were the Lord's, and I was one of His stewards. When I went to Kirtland, I had not a coat in the world, for previous to this I had given away everything I possessed, that I might be free to go forth and proclaim the plan of salvation to the inhabitants of the earth. Neither had I a shoe to my feet, and I had to borrow a pair of pants and a pair of boots. I staid [*sic*] there five years, and accumulated five thousand dollars. How

do you think I accomplished this? Why, the Lord Almighty gave me those means. . . . Ask an apostate, if they can, in truth, bear testimony to such a thing. They cannot do it (Brigham Young, *Journal of Discourses*, 2:128). [1853]

President Harold B. Lee, as one of the great contributors to the Welfare program of the Church, expressed an exalted view of how the Saints are to prosper materially and spiritually:

The Lord has clearly marked the way by which the "saints" or members of his Church are to be provided: "This is the way that I, the Lord, have decreed to provide for my saints, that the poor shall be exalted, in that the **rich** are made low. If any man shall take of the abundance which I have made, and impart not his portion, according to the law of my gospel, unto the poor and the needy, he shall with the wicked, lift up his eyes in hell, being in torment." (D&C 104:15–18) . . . When we begin to think of those whom we would help as being useful for something instead of being object of pity, we will then begin to plan ways by which the wisdom of the aged, the tenderness of widowhood and the youthful vigor of the able-bodied might be utilized toward the solving of their own problems and for the blessing of the lives of those less fortunate than they (Harold B. Lee, *Decisions for Successful Living*, 203).

Ever the practical and wise observer of human nature, and of the Saints, Brigham Young offered some observations regarding the destiny of the **rich** and the poor in the kingdom:

If the poor had all the surplus of the **rich**, many of them would waste it on the lusts of the flesh, and destroy themselves in using it. For this reason the Lord does not require the **rich** to give all their substance to the poor. . . . A great many think that He told the young man to give away all that he had, but Jesus did not require any such thing, neither did he say so,

but simply, "distribute to the poor." If the poor knew
what to do with what they have, many, yea very
many, in this land would have all that is necessary to
make them comfortable (Brigham Young, *Journal of
Discourses*, 13:302). [1870]

If they had the privilege of dictating the affairs of
this people, or of any other, they would divide the substance of the **rich** among the poor, and make all what
they call equal. But the question would arise with me
at once, how long would they remain equal? Make the
rich and the poor of this community, or of any other,
equal by the distribution of their earthly substance,
and how long would it be before a certain portion of
them would be calling upon the other portion, for something with which to sustain themselves? (Brigham
Young, *Discourses of Brigham Young*, 12:56, 317).

Elder Milton R. Hunter reminds us of the solemn responsibility that we each have in providing our **riches** to the
poor and the needy:

It is one of the vital laws of the gospel, as
revealed by the Lord in the latter days, for all church
members to provide for the poor that dwell among
them. In eighteen different revelations recorded in the
Doctrine and Covenants, Jesus Christ declared to
members of his church his will on this subject. The following extracts are typical of these revelations:

"And behold, thou will remember the poor, and
consecrate of thy properties for their support. . . . And
inasmuch as ye impart of your **substance** to the poor,
ye will do it unto me . . ." (D&C 42:30–31).

"Behold, I (the Lord) say unto you, that ye must
visit the poor and the needy and administer to their
relief, that they may be kept until all things may be
done according to my law which ye have received"
(D&C 44:6).

"And remember in all things the poor and the
needy, the sick and the afflicted, for he that doth not

> these things the same is not my disciple." (D&C
> 52:40).
>
> "therefore, if any man shall take of the **abun-
> dance** which I have made, and impart not his portion,
> according to the law of my gospel, unto the poor and
> the needy, he shall, with the wicked, lift up his eyes in
> hell, being in torment" (D&C 104:18).
>
> "Wo unto you **rich men**, that will not give your
> substance to the poor, for your **riches** will canker your
> souls; and this shall be your lamentation in the day of
> tribulation, and of judgment, and of indignation: The
> harvest is past, the summer is ended, and my soul is
> not saved" (D&C 56:16) (Milton R. Hunter, *Will a Man
> Rob God?*, 233).

While the Lord has promised us all that he has, if we
are true and faithful to the commandments and our covenants; there are dangers that in our temporal condition, we
will not endure well **prosperity and riches.** This is certainly
the lesson we can observe from the history of mankind,
particularly in the Book of Mormon. When we have needs,
we are more likely to be humble and responsive to the counsel of the Lord and Church leaders. When we have these
needs and wants satisfied, we are less likely to seek the
Lord in prayer, but rely on our own resources and abilities.
Thus, we turn to the arm of the flesh, thinking that we have
sufficient to achieve our goals and to care for ourselves.

Evidently this danger existed in the days after the pioneers came to Utah, because Elder George Q. Cannon cau-
tioned the Saints in 1873:

> But there is something that I dread more than
> active persecution. We have endured persecutions
> which have driven us from our homes. Mobs have
> burned our houses, destroyed our corn and wheat
> fields, and torn down our fences; our men have been
> slain, and in some instances our women ravished. We
> have been driven as wild beasts are driven from the
> habitations of men, and compelled to flee to the

wilderness. We have endured this, and we know that we can endure it, and live in the midst of it, for we have been tested. But we have not yet endured **prosperity,** we have not yet been tested in this crucible, which is one of the severest to which a people can be subjected. We have not been tested with **abundance** of property and wealth lavished upon us; and here, my brethren and sisters, is the point against which we have to guard more than all others, for there is more danger today to the Zion of God in the **wealth** that is pouring into and increasing in the hands of the Latter-day Saints . . . and I expect that there will be attractions stronger than the Gospel to hypocrites and those weak in the faith in the present phase of our history, and that influences now operating will produce the same results as we have witnessed, that is, to cleanse the people of God (George Q. Cannon, *Journal of Discourses* [1873], 15:298–299).

The prophet of our day, Gordon B. Hinckley, echoes this concern:

"It is our duty to preach the gospel, gather Israel, pay our tithing and build temples. The worst fear that I have about this people is that they will get **rich** in this country, forget God and His people, **wax fat,** and kick themselves out of the Church and go to hell (That is a quotation!) This people will stand mobbing, robbing, poverty, and all manner of persecution, and be true. But my greater fear for them is that they cannot stand **wealth**; and yet have to be tried with **riches,** for they will become the **richest people** on this earth." (Autobiography of James Brown, p. 119–23, cited by Preston Nibley, *Brigham Young, the Man and His Work,* p. 127–28) I would like to say that we are a **very rich** and blessed people" (Gordon B. Hinckley, *Teachings of Gordon B. Hinckley,* 443).

One of the great tests of faith for some Latter-day Saints is the paying a tithe of their incomes. This is more true, if the practice of it is not acquired, and recognized, early in life. Perhaps it is easier for children to pay one tenth of their income, because their parents take care of all of their needs and wants. So the parting of a dime from the dollar of allowance or from tasks performed is not difficult, and there is still ninety cents to spend or save.

Bishop Newell K. Whitney wrote in December 1844:

> Why did the Savior say, "how hardly shall they that have **riches** enter the kingdom of heaven?" Just converse with a **rich man** upon the subject of tithing, and you will soon see a reason why the **rich** can hardly enter the kingdom of heaven. When you converse with a man who has got ten thousand dollars in money in his hands, and tell him that his tithing will be one thousand dollars in money, you generally will see the force of the words of Jesus. That man would consider himself almost ruined if he should donate his one thousand dollars, whereas a man who has only ten dollars in money in the world, will come forward with cheerfulness and donate his tenth with joy. Remember the widow with her two mites (Newell K. Whitney, *History of the Church*, 7:320).

Elder Milton R. Hunter supports this idea that it harder to part with a tenth for those who have greater incomes:

> Many **wealthy men** in the Church pay an honest tithing and in all other respects they are good Latter-day Saints; however, others are affected by their **wealth**. Their hearts are set upon the things of this world; and the **richer** they become the more selfish they are.
>
> Latter-day prophets have also borne witness to the fact that it is difficult for certain **rich men** to part with their earthly possessions and pay an honest tithe unto the Lord. For example, President Brigham Young made the following observation:
>
> It is very true that the poor pay their tithing better than the **rich** do. If the **rich** would pay their tithing we should have plenty. The poor are faithful and prompt in paying their tithing, but the **rich** can hardly

afford to pay theirs—they have too much. If he has only ten dollars he can pay one; if he has only one dollar he can pay ten cents; it does not hurt him at all. If he has a hundred dollars he can possibly pay ten. If he has a thousand dollars he looks over it a little and says, "I guess I will pay it; it ought to be paid anyhow;" and he manages to pay his ten dollars or his hundred. But suppose a man is wealthy enough to pay ten thousand, he looks that over a good many times and says, "I guess I will wait until I get a little more, and then I will pay a good deal." And they wait and wait, like an old gentleman in the East; he waited and waited and waited to pay his tithing until he went out of the world, and this is the way with a great many. They wait and continue waiting, until, finally, the character comes along who is called Death, and he slips up to them and takes away their breath, then they are gone and cannot pay their tithing, they are too late, and so it goes (Milton R. Hunter, *Will a Man Rob God?* 139).

It seems that human nature had not changed much from the time of Brigham Young to that of President Heber J. Grant. The latter Prophet also observed that it was extremely difficult for **rich men** to deal honestly with the Lord. To quote:

"I know people of my own personal acquaintance that were honest, conscientious tithe payers when they were making three thousand, four thousand, five thousand, six thousand a year. But when, in the providence of the Lord, they made ten thousand or twenty thousand, they never grew an inch above that $600.00 a year tithing. They were just like grandfather's clock, stopped, never to go again.

"**Prosperity** distorted their vision. They could see what they were giving the Lord, but not what the Lord had given them.

"I know one man who paid $600.00 a year tithing. Being in the banking business and having available financial statements of many people, I knew that he made a little more than $45,000 that year, instead of the $6,000 which his tithing indicated. If he made $45,000 and paid $4,500 tithing, what would he have left? Over $40,000. If he had the right vision his heart should almost have burst with gratitude to God for the difference, rather than dwell upon the amount of tithing to be paid. . . . The more he made, the easier it should have been to pay his tithing. But no, he had set his heart on accumulating **money**" (Milton R. Hunter, *Will a Man Rob God?* 141).

President Joseph F. Smith spoke often and with great conviction concerning the principle and blessing of tithing by the faithful:

By this principle it shall be seen whose hearts are set on doing the will of God and keeping his commandments. . . . In this respect it is as essential as faith in God, as repentance of sin, as baptism for the remission of sin, or as the laying on of hands for the gift of the Holy Ghost. . . . But when a man keeps all the law that is revealed, according to his strength, his substance, and his ability, though what he does may be little, it is just as acceptable in the sight of God as if he were able to do a thousand times more (Joseph F. Smith, *Conference Report*, April 1900, 47–48).

While the payment of tithing and fast offerings evidence the faithfulness of Church members, there is another dimension of one's understanding of the second great commandment—to love our neighbors as ourselves. We are under the solemn personal duty to seek out the poor and the needy, the widow and the orphan, the sick and the afflicted. When we have found them, we are to administer to their needs and wants.

Many of the needs of our neighbors do not involve money or goods. What they may need most is someone to listen to their concerns and hopes. Perhaps they have some appliance that needs repair or a strong arm to lift boxes or furniture for them. Maybe a widow wants a priesthood blessing, or the sick who can't go to purchase some food or medicine. Could an expert in accounting or law counsel a young couple with irate creditors threatening them? Could an older couple who have endured a lifetime of challenges give some encouragement and direction to a young husband and wife who are experiencing contention and anger in their relationship?

The list of adversity and temptations that afflict us is almost endless, as we strive to endure to the end. As true Saints, we need to be anxiously engaged in giving our **riches**—time, energy, talents, and all with which the Lord has blessed us—to the Church of Jesus Christ of Latter-day Saints for the building up of the kingdom of God on the earth, and for the establishment of Zion—that we may be a Zion people.

Intellectual Superiority

In all ages and places there have been those who rejoiced in their **superiority**, be it talents, wealth, heritage, nationality, education, race, physical beauty, or titles. The narrative of the Book of Mormon is replete with such examples. All too frequently the history of civilizations and religions is founded in the **superiority** of their particular adherents, credos and practices.

Especially alarming are the personal relationships where one with **superior intellect** captures and directs the souls of others. Often that **intellect** believes that his, or her, way is best and should be blindly followed by their disciples.

In Church history, men such as Sidney Rigdon, Oliver Cowdery, William Law, William Godbe and his associates, and Samuel Brannan were persuaded by the adversary to reach for glory and power, or to "steady the ark." The lure of status and power is intoxicating to the **egos** of "almost all men, as soon as they get a little authority, as they suppose, they will immediately begin to exercise unrighteous dominion" (D&C 121:39).

Intellectual superiority is a product of pride. The first and greatest practitioner of it was Lucifer. He was **intelligent,** even the Son of the Morning, who came before Elohim, saying, "Behold, here am **I**, send **me**, **I** will be thy son, and **I** will redeem all mankind . . . and surely **I** will do it, wherefore give **me** thine honor" (Pearl of Great Price, Moses, 4:1).

In our dispensation Oliver Cowdery commanded the poorly educated Joseph Smith to correct the wording in a revelation (D&C 20). At a later time he declared that the Church would fail without his (Cowdery's) leadership. Sidney Rigdon, an eloquent and gifted man, shared with Prophet Joseph the glorious vision of the three degrees of glory (D&C 76). He determined to take over the leadership from Joseph, as he believed that he possessed greater talents and ability than the younger Prophet.

In the 1870s Orson Pratt described the subversion by a group of English **intellectuals** led by William Godbe. They conspired to correct the "drift" of the Church, and particularly the direction of Brigham Young, proclaiming that the Church had departed from spiritual manifestations, such as speaking in tongues, visions, miracles, healings, etc.:

> You have no doubt heard and reflected upon what is termed a very great and wonderful "movement"—something that is going to build up Zion in purity, taking place in our midst. The "movement" was commenced by a few individuals who had been cut off by the highest authority of the Church . . . and expelled because of teaching and publishing things contrary to the order of this Church. . . . I have seen Messrs. W.S. Godbe and E.L.T. Harrison once they were cut off from the church . . . they were so wrapt up in Spiritualism . . . related to me their **supernatural** manifestations . . . they said that Joseph Smith came to them, that Peter, James and John came to them; they also said that Jesus came to them, and that Solomon came to them, he said that he never had any concubines, but that all his women . . . were his wives. . . . Did they see any of these personages? Both of them say they saw none of them; it was merely a voice that they heard. They pretended to have seen a light when Jesus came but no personage (Orson Pratt, *Journal of Discourses*, 13:74). [1869]

Some members have become narrowly focused on a single principle or practice, often claiming a **superior**

knowledge of its efficacy in living the Gospel. President Gordon B. Hinckley expressed concern about such persons:

> Now and then I have watched a man become obsessed with a narrow segment of knowledge, I have worried about him. I have seen a few such. They have pursued relentlessly only a sliver of knowledge until they have lost a sense of balance. I think of two who went so far and became so misguided in their narrow pursuits, that they who once had been effective teachers of youth have been found to be in apostasy and have been excommunicated from the Church. Keep balance in our lives. Beware of obsession. Beware of narrowness (Gordon B. Hinckley, *Teachings of Gordon B. Hinckley,* 32).

Another type of **intellectual** in the Church may be those who refuse to fully participate in new revelation (counsel from the General Authorities), insisting that which they have is sufficient. In January 1858 George A. Smith told an audience in the Tabernacle:

> Trace over the history of apostates, and you will find that in almost every instance they lay down a standard rule—that is to say, "Thus far will we go, and no farther." For instance, we will take the Bible, Book of Mormon, and Doctrine and Covenants, and say concerning them, "They are true—the rule and guide of our faith and practice, they are the law we must abide, and we must go no farther;" and so their light is blown out. . . . This much we receive and no more. . . . We cut off the channel of revelation" (George A. Smith, *Journal of Discourses,* 6:160–61). [1858]

Those claiming **intellectual superiority** usually engage those whom they consider to be of lesser ability in argument over doctrine, authority or church practices. They **criticize** the errors and shortcomings of Joseph and Brigham and Wilford, to prove the inadequacy and fallibility of those great men, who were not perfect by their own admission. Joseph invited his critics, "If you will throw a cloak over my sins, I will over yours."

These superior critics are fond of debate, especially when they direct the exchange, and on a pet subject that they have researched beforehand. They seek out their victims with special attention, to establish the facts and logic of their argument. President Spencer W. Kimball had hard words for such hypocrites, citing particularly their reliance on **intellect** without the discernment of the Spirit:

> A prevalent form of rebellion is the "**higher criticism**" which is the delight of those Church members who become proud of their **intellectual powers**. Reveling in their supposed **superiority** they argue back and forth, analyze with their **unaided intellect** what can only be discerned by the eye of faith, and challenge and debunk such Church doctrines and policies as do not pass their **critical examination**. In all this they undermine the faith of those less qualified in knowledge and logic, sometimes apparently gaining pleasure from this result. . . . One punishment for the rebel against truth is that he loses the power to perceive the truth (Spencer W. Kimball, *Miracle of Forgiveness*, 45).

President Kimball also identified those who love to debate the gospel, or anything else that comes along:

> Another aspect of false witness is the "debate" . . . the **egoist** who feels to debate and argue every situation. . . . He will fight hard and long to gain a point regardless of where truth stands. There are those who argue even the wrong side in order to win the debate (Spencer W. Kimball, *Miracle of Forgiveness*, 53).

Elder Hugh B. Brown warns us in our day of events and dangers that will come, or that may be occurring in our time. Note that he points us to the prophecies of the New Testament. We are blessed to have prophets who declare God's warnings to us about the temptations and false teachers we face:

But there were false prophets also among the people, even as there shall be false teachers among you, who privily shall bring in **damnable heresies**, even denying the Lord that brought them, and bring upon themselves swift destruction (2 Pet. 2:1).

Let no man deceive you by any means: for that day shall not come, except there come a falling away first, and that man of sin be revealed, the son of perdition; Who opposeth and **exalteth** himself above all that is called God, or that is worshipped: so that he as God sitteth in the temple of God, shewing himself that he is God (2 Thes. 2:1–4).

President James E. Faust has given us a grave warning of the dangers in our day of the worldly temptations that we will face, which will whisper to us that they are better, or **superior**, to that which we have embraced:

The Spirit's voice is ever-present, but it is calm. The adversary tries to smother this voice with a multitude of loud, persistent, persuasive, and appealing voices:

Murmuring voices that conjure up perceived injustices.

Whining voices that abhor challenge and work.

Seductive voices offering sensual enticements.

Soothing voices that lull us into carnal security.

Intellectual voices that profess sophistication and scholarly **superiority**.

Proud voices that rely on the arm of flesh.

Flattering voices that puff us up with **pride.**

Cynical voices that destroy hope.

Entertaining voices that promote pleasure seeking.

In your generation you will be barraged by multitudes of voices telling you how to live, how to gratify your passions, how to have it all. You will have up to five hundred television channels at your fingertips.

There will be all sorts of software, interactive computer modems, databases, and bulletin boards; there will be desktop publishing, satellite receivers, and communications networks that will suffocate you with information. Local cable news networks will cover only local news. Everyone will be under more scrutiny. There will be fewer places of refuge and serenity. You will be bombarded with evil and wickedness like no other generation. As I contemplate this prospect, I am reminded of T.S. Eliot's words, "Where is the wisdom we have lost in knowledge? Where is the knowledge we have lost in information?"

Without question some will be deceived and will endure lives of heartbreak and sadness. Others will enjoy the promise recorded by Jeremiah, "I will put my law in their inward parts." (Jeremiah 31:33) In some ways it will be harder to be faithful in your day, perhaps in some ways even more challenging than pulling a handcart across the plains. When someone died in the wilderness of frontier America, their physical remains were buried and the handcarts continued west, but the mourning survivors had hope for their loved one's eternal soul. However, when someone dies spiritually in the wilderness of sin, hope may be replaced by dread and fear for the loved one's eternal welfare (James E. Faust, *Finding Light in a Dark World*, 98).

It is puzzling that those claiming **intellectual acumen** fail to recognize that spiritual matters are discerned by the Spirit. Doubtless, many who feel they are **intellectually superior**, have never experienced the influence of the Holy Spirit. But those who have experienced the light and its manifestations, should know better than to claim personal credit or exclusivity for spiritual truths. They should recall when they sought understanding of gospel matters, the fullness of truth came only after the Spirit had enhanced their **intellect**.

The fruit of the intellect is pride; whereas the fruit of the spirit is peace and joy.

TRIFLING AFFAIRS

What is that which turns people away from this Church? Very **trifling affairs** are generally the commencement of their divergence from the right path. If we follow a compass, the needle of which does not point correctly, a very slight deviation in the beginning will lead us, when we have traveled some distance, far to one side of the true point for which we are aiming (*Discourses of Brigham Young*, 83).

There are so many trivial offenses, deliberate or unintentional, that have caused Church members to become unhappy and/or justified in withdrawing from Church fellowship. A list of such incidents is endless: mispronouncing names, calling to or releasing persons from Church callings, chastisement for sins or mistakes, commenting on another's appearance, observing shortcomings of other members, gossiping, disagreement in class discussions, failure to greet or recognize other members, misunderstood gestures, exclusion from parties or meetings, criticism of a sermon or assignment or children's behavior, failure to express thanks, etc.

The aforementioned, and many others, may have occurred in most congregations or wards. So many of them may have been unintentional, or given out of awkwardness or shyness. One thing is sure, if we have a chip on our shoulder, it is easy to be offended.

Symonds Ryder was an early convert in Kirtland, who was called to serve as a missionary. When he received his missionary certificate from Church leaders, he noted that his name was spelled RIDER. He rejected the call and his membership, saying: "If the Spirit through which I have been called to preach could err in the matter of spelling my name, it might have erred in calling me to the ministry as well."

A most notorious case of a **trifling** matter involved the wife of Thomas B. Marsh, then President of the Twelve Apostles. Elder George A. Smith recounted the Marshes' affair in the April 1856 General Conference:

> The wife of Thomas B. Marsh, who was then President of the Twelve Apostles, and sister Harris concluded they would exchange milk, in order to make a little larger cheese than they otherwise could. To be sure to have justice done, it was agreed that they should not save the strippings (the extra-creamy milk that comes during the last part of milking a cow), but that the milk and strippings should all go together. Small matters to talk about here, to be sure, two women's exchanging milk to make cheese.
>
> Mrs. Harris, it appeared, was faithful to the agreement and carried to Mrs. Marsh the milk and strippings, but Mrs. Marsh, wishing to make some extra good cheese, saved a pint of strippings from each cow and sent Mrs. Harris the milk without the strippings.
>
> Finally it leaked out that Mrs. Marsh had saved strippings, and it became a matter to be settled by the (home) Teachers. They began to examine the matter, and it was proved that Mrs. Marsh had saved the strippings and consequently had wronged Mrs. Harris out of that amount.
>
> An appeal was taken from the Teacher to the Bishop, and a regular Church trial was had. President Marsh did not consider that the Bishop had done him and his lady justice, for they decided that the strippings were wrongfully saved, and that the woman had violated her covenant. Marsh immediately took an appeal to the High Council, who investigated the

question with much patience, and I assure you they were a grave body. Marsh being extremely anxious to maintain the character of his wife, as he was the President of the Twelve Apostles, and a great man in Israel, made a desperate defense, but the High Council finally confirmed the Bishop's decision.

Marsh, not being satisfied, took an appeal to the First Presidency of the Church, and Joseph and his Counselors had to sit upon the case, and they approved the decision of the High Council. This little affair, you will observe, kicked up a considerable breeze, and Thomas B. Marsh then declared that he would sustain the character of his wife, even if he had to go to hell for it.

The then President of the Twelve Apostles, the man who should have been first to do justice and cause reparation to be made for wrong, committed by any member of his family, took that position, and what next? He went before the magistrate and swore that the "Mormons" were hostile towards the State of Missouri.

That affidavit brought from the government of Missouri an exterminating order, which drove some 15,000 Saints from their homes and habitations, and some thousands perished through suffering the exposure consequent on this state of affairs (*Journal of Discourses*, 3:283–84). [1856]

Elder George A. Smith recalled the following incidents that involved **trifling** matters but with disastrous consequences:

I recollect when I first began to discern the operation of the spirit of apostasy. . . . One of the men (Norman A. Brown) lost a horse. "Now," said he, "is it possible that this is the work of God? If this had been the work of God, my horse would not have died when I was going to Zion."

Joseph H. Wakefield, who baptized me, . . . had absolutely seen the Prophet come down from the room where he was engaged in translating the word of God, and actually go to playing with the children! This convinced him that the Prophet was not a man of God, and that the work was false.

> Doctor P. Hurlburt . . . in consequence of improper conduct among females . . . was expelled from the Church. He confessed his wickedness to the Council. He promised before God, angels and men that he would . . . live his religion and preserve his integrity, if they would only forgive him. The Council forgave him; but Joseph told him, "You are not honest in this confession." A few days afterwards he published his renunciation of the work, assigning as a reason, that he deceived that Council . . . when he only confessed to see whether the Council had power to discern his spirit (George A. Smith, *Journal of Discourses*, 7:114). [1858]

Pride so frequently enters into trivial incidents that set members off on the path to apostasy. With hurt pride, one may then criticize their Bishop or other leaders for allowing such goings on. Or, they lose the calming influence of the Spirit. It is then easy for a person to revive and magnify small items of doctrine or Church practice that heretofore had lain dormant or of no consequence in his mind; now this "mote" becomes a "beam" in the eyes of the offended.

In the early days of the Church, converts came from diverse religious beliefs, and from foreign lands where traditions were strange. As they came together in congregations of Zion, it was easy for misunderstandings to arise. When words and deeds were contrary to those of other converts, or from the developing codes of conduct of the restored Church, the potential for conflict and wounded egos was huge.

To survive the requirements of this new latter-day culture, and the temptations that Satan heaped upon these converts, they needed a great endowment of the Spirit, and its gifts. Visions of angels, healings of the sick and crippled, missionary successes, were just some of the blessings that were showered upon the faithful. However, not everyone was so blessed, and many who were blessed, were overcome by the cares of the world and the temptations of the adversary.

Brigham Young was one of those whose testimony was so firm that he never looked back, after his two-year examination of the Book of Mormon and the doctrines of the restored gospel. He counseled the Saints on various occasions to patiently and openly resolve their differences with fellow Saints and neighbors:

> I wish men would look upon that eternity which is before them. In the great morning of the resurrection, with what grief would they look upon their little **trifling affairs** of this probation; they would say, "O! Do not mention it, for it is a source of mortification to me to think that I ever should be guilty of doing wrong, or of neglecting to do good to my fellow men, even if they have abused me" (Brigham Young, *Journal of Discourses*, 1:32). [1852]

> When a difference of judgment exists between two parties, let them come together and lay their difficulties at each other's feet, laying themselves down in the cradle of humility, and say, "Brother (or sister) I want to do right; yea, I will even wrong myself, to make you right." Do you not think that a man or woman, acting in that manner towards his or her neighbor, would be justified by the law of righteousness? Their judgments come together, and they are agreed: there would, consequently, be no need of calling in a third person to settle the difference. After taking this course, if you cannot come together, then call in a third person and settle it (Brigham Young, *Journal of Discourses*, 6:319). [1852]

> Contentions frequently arise to so alienating a degree that brethren have no faith in each other's honesty and integrity, when, perhaps, both parties have stumbled over a little, selfish, ignorant, personal misunderstanding, are carrying it to the extent of wishing

to cut each other off from the Church. Very frequently such cases are presented before me. Unravel the difficulty, and it is found to have started in a **trifling** misunderstanding in relation to some small matter; all the trouble has arisen from a most frivolous cause. Avoid nursing misunderstandings into difficulties. Some talk with a heavy, deep stress upon their words, without intending anything harsh or unkind (Brigham Young, *Journal of Discourses* [1877], 8:72).

If your neighbors talk about you, and you think that they do wrong in speaking evil of you, do not let them know that you ever heard a word, and conduct yourselves as if they always did right, and it will mortify them, and they will say, "We'll not try this game any longer" (Brigham Young, *Journal of Discourses,* 19:70). [1877]

Let us make ourselves capable of doing at least a little good, and this will occupy our minds upon something that is indeed profitable to others, and will somewhat divert our attention from worshipping ourselves and blaming everybody that does not do the same (Brigham Young, *Journal of Discourses,* 10:205). [1863]

We could well follow Joseph Smith's appeal to the Saints:

If you will throw a cloak of charity over my sins,
I will over yours.

To avoid the many **trifling matters** that might arise in our lives, especially those that involve our Church activity, we need to stay focused upon that which matters most:

- our testimony of the gospel
- keeping our covenants and the commandments
- retaining the Holy Spirit.

PRIDE

Our day has been called the "me generation," wherein we are focused upon satisfying personal wants NOW. The hero-worship of professional athletes, movie and television stars, political leaders and business moguls has infected young and old alike. This ego-conscious environment has been further magnified by the expansion of instantaneous information in the form of television, cable, computers and the internet.

Although astronomic salaries and the power to influence by these new "heroes" are obvious allurements, the hidden and primal attraction to all fans or aspirants of the "high and mighty" is personal fame, egotism, and adulation—all expressions of **pride.**

Almost all of the causes of apostasy that are presented in previous chapters of this book are derived from the **pride** of the apostates. For that matter, each of us is confronted daily with situations and relationships that deal with potential consequences of **pride**.

Teaching and nurturing children and youth to have self-esteem and to be self-sufficient demands that we help them to achieve self-confidence. God has decreed that we aspire to God-hood; an achievement that requires great vision, great commitment and great performance, all of which carry the seeds of **pride** for the unwary and undisciplined.

I recall vividly of hearing President Ezra Taft Benson teach us about **pride** in the April 1989 General Conference.

My profound impression then of the truth of his sermon has been reinforced with this writing. He told us that:

> the central feature of **pride** is enmity—enmity toward God and enmity toward our fellowmen. Enmity means "hatred toward, hostility to, or a state of opposition." It is the power by which Satan wishes to reign over us.
>
> **Pride** is essentially competitive in nature. We pit our will against God's. When we direct our **pride** toward God, it is in the spirit of "my will and not thine be done." Our will in competition to God's will allows desires, appetites, and passions to go unbridled.
>
> Our enmity toward God takes on many labels, such as rebellion, hardheartedness, stiff-neckedness, unrepentant, puffed up, easily offended, and sign seekers. The **proud** wish God would agree with them. They aren't interested in changing their opinions to agree with God's (Ezra Taft Benson, *Ensign*, May 1989).

Author Robert J. Mc Cracken warns:

> If we make a listing of our sins, [**pride**] . . . is the one that heads the list, breeds all the rest, and does more to estrange us from our neighbors or from God than any evil we can commit. . . . In this aspect, it is not only the worst of the seven deadly sins; it is the parent sin, the one that leads to every other, the sin from which no one is free (Arthur McCracken, *What Is Sin? What Is Virtue?* 11–13).

Apostle Neal A. Maxwell suggests some of the diverse dimensions of **pride**:

> Just as meekness is in all our virtues, so **pride** is in all our sins. . . . Henry Fairlie, in writing of the pervasiveness of **pride**, observed that it is "an assertion of self-sufficiency—a denial of one's need for community with others, which is in fact a form of selfishness, since it is always accompanied by a refusal of one's obligation of community with others." Fairlie also observed that **pride** "is a sin of neglect: It causes us to

ignore others. It is a sin of aggression: It provokes us to hurt others. It is a sin of condescension: It makes us patronize others."

One reason to be particularly on guard against **pride** is that "the devilish strategy of **pride** is that it attacks us, not in our weakest points, but in our strongest. It is preeminently the sin of the noble mind" (Neal A. Maxwell, *Meek and Lowly*, 50).

President Benson gives us another aspect of **pride**:

The **proud** make every man their adversary by pitting their intellects, opinions, works, wealth, talents, or any other worldly measuring device against others. In the words of C.S. Lewis: "**Pride** gets no pleasure out of having something, only out of having more of it than the next man. . . . It is the comparison that makes you **proud**: the pleasure of being above the rest. Once the element of competition has gone, pride has gone" (*Mere Christianity*, 109–10) (Ezra Taft Benson, *Ensign*, May 1989, 4).

Pride existed from the beginning, its author brought it from the Council in Heaven. In that Lucifer's "plan of salvation" was merely a ruse to gain the power and glory of the Father, it was the supreme act of **pride**. His arrogance is particularly brazen, inasmuch as Elohim in his omniscience would have known fully of Lucifer's real intentions.

While Lucifer's deception failed in heaven, as Satan he has promoted **pride** in its myriad forms with great success on earth. Most of the great wars and persecutions have been caused by offenses, illogical or misunderstood, in the name of honor, national or racial pride. The atrocities of the Nazis in World War II and more recently in the ethnic cleansing in Yugoslavia and Ruanda are reminders of the tragedies caused by **pride.**

Elder Maxwell describes the iniquities of Sodom from the Old Testament:

I have never seen **pride** as fierce or as unjustified as the **pride** of the Sodomites. They were **proud** of their riches, they were proud of their wealth, they were **proud** of their injustice toward men. They were even **proud** of their **pride**.

Beneath their **proud** outward face, however, there was seen in the faces of the inhabitants of Sodom boredom and hatred of self. Because they no longer loved their God or their fellowmen, they had grown to hate life and to hate themselves. But the more fiercely they disliked life, the more fiercely did they seem to cling to it. They seemed to seek out the sensations—those things that would convince them they were still alive—and these were the most selfish vices (Neal A. Maxwell, *Look Back at Sodom*, 8).

Elder Maxwell also reviews the interesting and eventually positive case of Jonah, who **pridefully** disobeyed the Lord:

Jonah sought to avoid going to Nineveh when he was called, seeking instead to go to Tarshish. Yet it was in Nineveh that he received one of the great lessons of his life that provided such an insight for us all. The meek will go where they are called; their obedience will see them through when reason and past experiences, by themselves, are not enough to sustain them. There are on record more examples of individuals who have meekly turned around in response to a call to serve or to repent or to follow divine instruction than examples of groups doing such. Nineveh, however, is a dramatic exception to the pattern, as are some brief turnarounds in the Book of Mormon. It is a heroic thing for individuals to reverse themselves, their attitudes, and their patterns of behavior in order to pursue discipleship; it is truly remarkable for a whole people to do so (Neal A. Maxwell, *Meek and Lowly*, 55–56).

In the Book of Mormon we find a wealth of examples of the calamities of **prideful** people, probably rooted in the rebellious DNA of Laman and Lemuel and their descendants. President Harold B. Lee recounts a prophet's warning to the Nephites who had **pride** in their hearts because of their ease and their exceeding great prosperity:

> "Yea, and we may see at the very time when he doth prosper his people. . . . Yea, then is the time that they do harden their hearts, and do forget the Lord their God, and do trample under their feet the Holy One—Yea, and this because of their ease, and their exceedingly great prosperity" (Hel. 12:2).

> "Yea, how quick to be lifted up in **pride**; yea, how quick to boast, and to all manner of that which is iniquity; and how slow are they to remember the Lord their God, and to give ear unto his counsels, yea, how slow to walk in wisdom's paths!" (Hel. 12:5) (Harold B. Lee, *Stand Ye in Holy Places*, 82).

Following the ministry of the resurrected Jesus in the land Bountiful, the Nephites lived in peace and righteousness for 200 years. Elder Jeffrey R. Holland tells what occurred after this long period of Zion existence:

> After two hundred years, the movement away from the Zion-like principles of Christ's teachings was inexorable: "There began to be among them those who were lifted up in **pride**, such as the wearing of costly apparel, and all manner of fine pearls, and of the fines things of the world. And from that time forth they did have their goods and their substance no more common among them. And they began to be divided into classes; and they began to build up churches unto themselves to get gain, and began to deny the true church of Christ."

> Although they "professed to know Christ," these false churches denied essential elements of the gospel, entertained wickedness within their ranks, "and did administer that which was sacred unto him to whom it had been forbidden because of unworthiness."

> These wicked ones, now again called Lamanites, began to build up the secret combinations of Gadianton.

But even more tragically, the righteous, those who had been called Nephites, "began to be **proud** in their hearts, because of their exceeding riches, and become vain like unto their brethren, the Lamanites." Thus both the people of Nephi and the new Lamanites became exceedingly wicked, one like unto another (Jeffrey R. Holland, *Christ and the New Covenant*, 315).

In the glorious Pentecostal season that occurred at the time of the dedication of the Kirtland Temple, to the Saints it seemed that they would enjoy the continued love and gifts of the Spirit. Elder B. H. Roberts explained how **pride** and its manifestations changed this idyllic atmosphere:

> For a time it appeared that the Saints would long enjoy the blessings of their temple and the communion and instruction of heavenly messengers. But not so.
>
> **Pride** and worldly-mindedness among the saints had preceded some of their financial difficulties, and when their troubles came thick upon them they accused each other of all kinds of sin and folly; there were evil surmisings, bickerings, fault-finding, false accusations and bitterness, until the spirit of the gospel in Kirtland was well nigh eclipsed. The Prophet especially was censured. It was reported that the "bank" had been "instituted by the will of God," i.e., by revelation, "and would never fail, let men do what they would." This the Prophet denied in open conference, saying that "if this had been declared no one had authority from him for doing so," and added that he "had always said that unless the institution was conducted on righteous principles it would not stand." Many, however, became disaffected toward the Prophet, "as though I were the sole cause."
>
> Matters went on from bad to worse, apostasy was rife even among some of the high church officials. Both Sidney Rigdon and the Prophet were compelled to flee the state for security of their personal safety from false brethren (B. H. Roberts, *Comprehensive History of the Church*, 1:402).

Of those men whom I have profiled, forty were either excommunicated or left the Church; almost all of them were caught up in some **prideful** situation that carried them off to apostasy. Some felt superior to the young Prophet. Others just would not humbly accept the word of the Lord, or counsel from the Prophet, but insisted on going their own way.

> I noticed when I was very young in the Church, that men who were greatly gifted of the Lord and had many manifestations, were the men who apostatized; with the exception of the Prophet Joseph Smith, nearly every one was overthrown. I suppose the reason of it was that they were lifted up in **pride** and allowed the adversary to take advantage of them. . . . I have seen Elders in my experience that when they got their own spirit moved very much they imagined that it was the Spirit of God, and it was difficult in some instances to tell the difference between the suggestions of their own spirit and the voice of the spirit of God (George Q. Cannon, *Journal of Discourses*, 22:104). [1880]

Oliver Cowdery was educated and intelligent. Elder George Q. Cannon tells of an occasion when this Second Elder was overcome in **pride**:

> While the Prophet, aided by his wife, was transcribing the revelations, he received a startling letter, couched in stern and disrespectful terms, addressed to him by Oliver from Fayette. The letter demanded that Joseph should erase certain words from one of the commandments given by God to the Church, alleging that they had been incorrectly written [D&C 20]. The Prophet was shocked and grieved, because he saw therein the snare which Satan had set for the feet of some of the flock of Christ. He knew, too, how prone Oliver was to be lifted up in the **pride** of his heart; and he saw in this a concession to evil by Oliver which must be checked and withdrawn, or Oliver, and those who had sympathy for him, would soon be cast out.

> Joseph wrote a letter, full of loving admonition, and yet rebuking firmly the error to which Oliver was yielding. Joseph informed him that the revelation had been correctly written—it was the command of God, and no man had authority to take from it a single word (George Q. Cannon, *Life of Joseph Smith the Prophet*, 91).

Brigham H. Roberts thrills at this following account of Martin Harris being chastised by the Lord through the Prophet Joseph:

> After attending to the usual services, namely, reading, singing, and praying, Joseph arose from his knees, and approaching Martin Harris with a solemnity that thrills through my veins to this day, when it occurs to my recollection, said: "Martin Harris, you have got to humble yourself before your God this day, that you may obtain a forgiveness of your sins. If you do, it is the will of God that you should look upon the plates, in company with Oliver Cowdery and David Whitmer."
>
> When the **pride**, egotism, and stubbornness of Martin Harris is taken into account, this preliminary admonition of the Prophet to him is eminently fitting and necessary and in harmony with all the circumstances of Martin's character and the subsequent facts to be related (B. H. Roberts, *New Witness for God*, 275).

William E. McLellin was a prominent leader in the Church in Kirtland. His ability and experience were greatly valued by the Lord, who called him as a member of the original Quorum of the Twelve. George Q. Cannon recalled a particular episode where McLellin's **pride** caused him to challenge the Prophet:

> McLellin was commanded to repent of some things and was warned against adultery, a sin to which, it appears, he was inclined. He was promised great blessings if he would overcome. This instruction, direct from the Almighty, seemed to affect him for a

time, but the words did not sink deep into his heart, because he soon rebelled and attempted to bring reproach upon the Church of Christ. He joined with others in whom the spirit of discontent was brooding to find fault with the revelations of the Lord which Joseph received.

When the Prophet returned to Hiram, the Lord condemned the folly and **pride** of McLellin and his sympathizers, and said to them that they might seek out of the Book of Commandments even the least of the revelations, and appoint the wisest among them to make one like unto it from his own knowledge. Filled with vanity and self-conceit, McLellin sacrilegiously essayed to write a commandment in rivalry of those bestowed direct from God upon the Church. But he failed miserably in his audacious effort, to the chagrin and humiliation of himself and his fellows. . . . The elders obeyed his (Joseph's) behest of the Lord and declared in strength and power their absolute knowledge that the revelations which had been bestowed upon the Church were from God (George Q. Cannon, *Life of Joseph Smith the Prophet,* 127).

Sidney Rigdon, who served for ten years as a Counselor to Joseph Smith, was given the following prophecy through the Prophet:

And again, blessed be Brother Sidney: notwithstanding he shall be **high** and **lifted up,** yet shall bow down under the yoke like unto an ass that Croucheth beneath his burden, that learneth his master's will by the stroke of the rod; thus saith the Lord: yet, the Lord will have mercy on him, and he shall bring forth much fruit . . . because of Him who putteth forth His hand, and lifteth him up out of deep mire, and pointeth him out the way, and guideth his feet when he stumbles, and humbleth him in his **pride**. Blessed are his generations: nevertheless one shall hunt after them as a man hunteth after an ass that has strayed in the wilderness, and straightway findeth him and bringeth him into the fold (Joseph Smith, *History of the Church,* 1:443).

119

Recall the behavior of William Smith, younger brother of Joseph, who was called as an apostle in the initial Quorum of the Twelve, but his service was filled with much tribulation and rebellion. Despite the promise of this prophecy, his **pride** and disobedience drove him to apostasy and disappointment to those who loved him:

> Brother William is as the fierce lion, which divideth not the spoil because of his strength, and in the **pride** of his heart he will neglect the more weighty matters until his soul is bowed down in sorrow; and then he shall return and call on the name of his God, and shall find forgiveness, and shall wax valiant, therefore, he shall be saved unto the uttermost; and as the roaring lion of the forest in the midst of his prey, so shall the hand of his generation be lifted up against those who are set on high, that fight against the God of Israel, fearless and undaunted shall they be in battle, in avenging the wrongs of the innocent, and relieving the oppressed; therefore, the blessings of the God of Jacob shall be in the midst of his house, notwithstanding his rebellious heart (Joseph Smith, *History of the Church*, 1:467).

Nephi's great vision of the Tree of Life included a portrayal of the "great and spacious building" that represented the **pride** of the world. The angel of the Lord told Nephi that this represented the world in the latter days—in our time.

This same Nephi was given another vision by the Lord of the days in which we live. Nephi prophesied concerning the wickedness that would prevail in the latter days and the corruption among the churches of the world. This corruption was brought about because they had not cared for the poor. Then he prophesied:

> Because of **pride**, and because of false teachers, and false doctrine, their churches have become corrupted, and their churches are lifted up; because of **pride** they are puffed up. They rob the poor because of their fine sanctuaries; they rob the poor because of

their fine clothing; and they persecute the meek and the poor in heart, because in their **pride** they are puffed up.

They wear stiff neck and high heads; yea, and because of **pride**, and wickedness, and abominations, and whoredoms, they have all gone astray save it be a few, who are the humble followers of Christ; nevertheless, they are led, that in many instances they do err because they are taught by the precepts of men.

O the wise, and the learned, and the rich, that are puffed up in the **pride** of their hearts, and all those who preach false doctrines, and all those who commit whoredoms, and pervert the right way of the Lord, wo, wo, wo be unto them, saith the Lord God Almighty, for they shall be thrust down to hell! (2 Ne. 28:12–15).

President Howard W. Hunter draws on a story from Luke in the New Testament to suggest two contrasting attitudes, one of which we may follow in a proper show of **pride**. He cites the Pharisee and a tax collector, and why they prayed as they did in the temple:

After the two men entered the temple, the Pharisee stood by himself, apart from the tax collector, and thanked God that he was "not as other men are, extortioners, unjust, adulterers" who fail to live the commandments of the law, "or even as this publican," he said. Though he was in form thanking God, his self-centered thoughts were on his own self-righteousness. In justification he added: "I fast twice in the week, I give tithes of all that I possess" (Luke 18:11–12). His prayer was not one of thankfulness, but of boastfulness.

The boastful spirit and **pride** of this Pharisee is not unlike that of Rabbi Simeon ben Jochai, mentioned in the Talmud, who said, "If there were only thirty righteous persons in the world, I and my son should make two of them; but if there were but twenty, I and my son would be of the number; and if there were but ten, I and my son would be of the number; and if there were but five, I and my son would be of the five; and if there were but two, I and my son would be those two; and if there were but one, myself should be that one" (*Bereshith Rabba,* s. 35, vol. 34).

The tax collector standing afar off, feeling the weight of his iniquities pressing down upon him, and being conscious of his sins and unworthiness to stand before God, cast his eyes to the ground and "would not lift up so much as his eyes unto heaven" when he prayed. In deep distress he beat upon his breast and pleaded, "God be merciful to me a sinner" (Luke 18:13).

Could there be greater contrast in the prayers of two men? The Pharisee stood apart because he believed he was better than other men, whom he considered as common. The publican stood apart also, but it was because he felt himself unworthy. The Pharisee thought of no one other than himself and regarded everyone else a sinner, whereas the publican thought of everyone else as righteous as compared with himself, a sinner. The Pharisee asked nothing of God but relied upon his own self-righteousness. The publican appealed to God for mercy and forgiveness of his sins.

Continuing the story, Jesus then said: "I tell you, this man, referring to the publican, the despised tax collector, went down to his house justified rather than the other" (Luke 18:14). In other words, the Lord said he was absolved, forgiven, or vindicated (Howard W. Hunter, *That We Might Have Joy,* 141).

Elder Carlos E. Asay counsels us regarding our prayers:

I fear that occasionally we allow "Rameumptom-like" practices to encroach upon our family prayers. This occurs when we offer "the self-same prayer unto God," use boastful language, display self-righteous **pride,** and become more concerned about form than substance (Alma 31:12–23). Satan came among the Zoramites "and tempted them to worship him" by perverting their order of prayer. We must not permit him to do the same to us (Carlos E. Asay, *Family Pecan Trees,* 16).

Elder Alexander B. Morrison points us to the warning by Nephi, and then by Moroni, who speaks to us as if we were present [with him]:

> "There began to be some disputings among the people; and some were lifted up unto **pride** and boastings because of their exceedingly great riches, yea, even unto great persecutions. . . . And the people began to be distinguished by ranks. . . . And thus there became a great inequality in all the land. . . . Now the cause of this iniquity of the people was this—Satan had great power, unto the stirring up of the people to do all manner of iniquity, and to the puffing them up with **pride**, tempting them to seek for power, and authority, and riches, and the vain things of the world" (3 Nephi 6:10–15).
>
> Lest we falsely believe that those circumstances applied uniquely to the Nephite church, it is well to keep in mind these somber words of Moroni, speaking to our generation and time: "Behold, I speak unto you as if ye were present, and yet ye are not. But behold, Jesus Christ hath shown you unto me, and I know your doing. And I know that ye do walk in the **pride** of your hearts; and there are none save a few only who do not lift themselves up in the **pride** of their hearts, unto the wearing of very fine apparel, unto envying, and strifes, and malice, and persecutions, and all manner of iniquities; and your churches, yea, even every one, have become polluted because of the **pride** of your hearts.
>
> "For behold, ye do love money, and your substance, and your fine apparel, and the adorning of your churches, more than ye love the poor and the needy, the sick and the afflicted" (Mormon 8:35–37) (Alexander B. Morrison, *Visions of Zion*, 11).

Elder George Q. Cannon observed that human nature may be manifest in deference, or even in adulation, of the rich, famous and powerful, but does not qualify one for Church position or callings:

123

The idea should never gain ground that the rich man in the Church is entitled to any more considera- tion than the humblest member. Men of superior virtues and powers, whether those virtues and pow- ers be represented in the ability to gain wealth, to acquire education, or to display genius and wisdom, will always occupy a commanding place in the social, the business, and religious world.

It is one thing, however, to respect wealth and its powers, and quite another to become mere syco- phants to it. Neither the Church, nor its blessings nor favors, have ever been, from its organization, submis- sive to or purchasable by the mammon of this world. No man need to hope that he can buy the gifts of God. Those who attempt to buy the treasures of heaven will perish, and their wealth will perish with them. Wealth may wield an undue influence and gain prestige in society, even though its possessor may be greatly wanting in moral worthiness. And being a power in itself, may be a danger through opportunities for cor- ruption and seduction. Those, therefore, who have lis- tened to the fallacious arguments of the advantages of wealth and its power, independent of virtue, have in store for them a great disappointment if they act upon any such false theories.

The trouble is, that young men are very apt to mistake a friendly and cordial greeting to those in possession of wealth for a genuine friendship and sin- cere confidence The unworthy rich should be as much the object of our pity as the unworthy poor. Those who imagine that wealth may be substituted for virtue are certainly doomed to disappointment; and yet men sometimes foolishly and enviously suggest that the highest social recommendation and religious standing as well as the sincere friendship of the pure in heart are subject to the command of the mammon of unright- eousness (George Q. Cannon, *Gospel Doctrine*, 117).

When one teaches a powerful lesson, or delivers an inspiring sermon, the compliments from appreciative members can be heady stuff. President Hugh B. Brown counsels all of us, including those in high places, to remember from whence our gifts and inspiration comes:

> Along that line I would like to quote what the Prophet Joseph Smith said, and this appeal has a warning admonition to all of us to beware of **pride,** to remember that our effectiveness and success will depend upon our humility and our dependence upon divine guidance.
>
> The Prophet said, "When the Twelve or any other witnesses stand before the congregations of the earth and they preach in the power and demonstration of the spirit of God, and the people are astonished and confounded at the doctrines and they say, 'That man has preached a powerful discourse, a great sermon,' then let that man or those men take care that they do not ascribe the glory unto themselves, but be careful that they are humble and ascribe the praise and glory to God and the Lamb. For it is by the power of the Holy Priesthood and the Holy Ghost that they have power thus to preach. Who art thou, O Man, but dust. And from whom receiveth thou thy power and blessings but from God" (Hugh B. Brown, *Continuing the Quest*, 61).

President Ezra Taft Benson adds counsel on the danger of ingratitude for our blessings:

> What a sin of ingratitude it would be if we should forget the Gracious Hand which has preserved us, enriched us, strengthened us. What a sin of **pride** if we should imagine, in our vanity, that our blessings were due to our own wisdom and virtue. What a grievous error it would be if we should become so filled with self-sufficiency as no longer to feel the need of prayer (Ezra Taft Benson, *So Shall We Reap*, 7).

President Benson declared that there is no such thing as **righteous pride.** So those joyous feelings we experience when our children, or others, speak or behave well can be expressed as gratitude for the Lord's blessings upon our loved ones and ourselves.

We are reminded of the quote attributed to St. Francis of Assisi, wherein he exclaimed, "Except for the grace of God, there go I." All of the intelligence and gifts that we possess come from God, our Eternal Father. He that giveth, can taketh away.

Illness or accident can reduce the most brilliant and gifted person to total dependency in a moment.

Well should we heed Proverbs 16:18: "**Pride** goeth before destruction, and an haughty spirit before a fall."

POLYGAMY

It is interesting that in my review of the scriptures and the writings of the General Authorities that there were not any references to **polygamy** as a cause of apostasy. Yet in my research of the lives of those early Saints that are profiled, and in other records, it was quite evident that the doctrine and practice of plural marriage in the Mormon Church precipitated controversy and apostasy.

The apostates in Nauvoo, many of whom had violated the teachings of the Prophet Joseph Smith regarding **plural marriage,** were ringleaders in the events that led to the martyrdom of Joseph and Hyrum Smith. These men—John C. Bennett, William and Wilson Law, Clarence and Francis Higbee, and Robert Foster—were reported to have engaged in adultery in the months preceding their excommunication and the martyrdom of the Smith brothers.

In the minds of many Saints in Nauvoo, there was a distinct conflict between the Book of Mormon (Jacob 2:24–30) and the revelation on plural marriage (D&C 132) given through the Prophet Joseph. Jacob instructed the Nephites that they were to have one wife, condemning David and Solomon for their multiple wives and concubines.

> Wherefore, I the Lord God, will not suffer that this people shall do like unto them of old. Wherefore, my brethren, hear me, and hearken to the word of the Lord; for there shall not any man among you have save it be one wife; and concubines he shall have none; for I, the Lord God delight in the chastity of women.

And whoredoms are an abomination before me; thus saith the Lord of Hosts (Jacob 2:27–28).

Brigham H. Roberts offers the following resolution to the dilemma:

> Here those desiring to show the conflict between this passage and the Nauvoo revelation on marriage close the quotation, and of course claim the victory for their contention. . . . The verse omitted from their data, reads: *"For if I will, saith the Lord of Hosts, raise up seed unto me, I will command my people; otherwise they shall hearken unto these things."* (Jacob 2:30). . . . God has given a law to the Nephites that a man should have but one wife, if for any special reason the Lord would vary from that system, he would command his people. . . . In other words the passage in Jacob may properly be regarded as a prophecy that such a change as indicated would be made, of which the Nauvoo revelation is the fulfillment (B. H. Roberts, *A Comprehensive History of the Church*, 2:108–9).

President Gordon B. Hinckley further clarifies the practice of plural marriage:

> To many people Mormonism has meant one thing only—**polygamy**. This has been the subject of lurid tales in all parts of the world. Once such stories were extremely popular. But as the facts have come to be known, such writings have largely disappeared.
>
> The truth of the matter is this: Mormonism claims to be a restoration of God's work in all previous dispensations. The Old Testament teaches that the patriarchs—those men favored of God in ancient times—had more than one wife under divine sanction. In the course of the development of the Church in the nineteenth century, it was revealed to the leader of the Church that such a practice of marriage again should be entered into.
>
> The announcement of this doctrine was a severe shock. Most of the converts to Mormonism were of

Puritan New England stock. Shortly after Brigham Young heard of the doctrine he saw a funeral cortege passing down the street, and he is reported to have said that he would gladly trade places with the man in the coffin rather than face this doctrine.

Nevertheless, the leaders of the Church accepted it as a commandment from God. It was not an easy thing to do. Only those whose characters were of the highest, and who had proved themselves capable of maintaining more than one family, were permitted so to marry. Never at any time were more than a small percentage of the families of the Church polygamous. The practice was regarded strictly as a religious principle (Gordon B. Hinckley, *Teachings of Gordon B. Hinckley*, 456).

Elder Francis M. Gibbons provides an insight into the reluctance that Joseph Smith dealt with in introducing the practice of **plural marriage** to the Church:

About the time of the April 1841 conference, Joseph Smith married his first plural wife. The revelation explaining the doctrine of plural marriage was recorded on July 12, 1843 (D&C 132), though Joseph had received it more than ten years earlier while working on the translation of the Bible. . . . Even in 1843, when it was put into writing, the revelation was not published and would not be published until years after the Prophet's death.

Because of his strict upbringing, Joseph Smith resisted entering into plural marriage. He did so only after being rebuked by the Lord. . . . Not being authorized to publicly discuss the revelation, yet under direction to teach and practice it privately, Joseph walked a narrow line.

Emma's acceptance of the doctrine of **plural marriage** did not come easily. Indeed, she rebelled at first. Later, she accepted it grudgingly, even to the extent of approving those whom her husband took as plural wives. After Joseph's death, however, she reverted to her rebellion to the point of denying her husband ever had engaged in **polygamy** (Francis M. Gibbons, *Dynamic Disciples*, 24–25).

Much confusion and tension was rampant in Nauvoo due to the secrecy surrounding the practice of **plural marriage.** At first it was the subject of gossip, only later to erupt in public conversation and condemnation. Those men who had been exposed for perverting the doctrine in adulterous activities accused Joseph and others of perfidy and hypocrisy. John C. Bennett was joined by William Law, another Counselor to the Prophet.

> Failing in his effort to persuade Joseph to abandon **polygamy,** he (William Law) and several conspirators plotted the Prophet's death. Joseph became suspicious. "What can be the matter with these men?" he asked rhetorically in his journal on January 5, 1844. "Is it that the wicked flee when no man pursueth . . . or that Presidents Law and Marks are absolutely traitors to the church . . . ? Can it be possible the traitor . . . is one of my quorum?" (Francis M. Gibbons, *Dynamic Disciples*, 27).

The controversy affected even the most faithful. Orson Pratt arrived in Nauvoo to find that his wife was embroiled in an accusation that she had been seduced by John C. Bennett. Bennett claimed that it was Joseph that had seduced sister Pratt. John Taylor told of members of the Quorum of the Twelve who labored with Orson in his dilemma, of the excommunication of Elder Pratt, and finally of his reconciliation with the Prophet and his reinstatement into the Church and the Quorum. But there were others who lost their confidence in Joseph and the leaders, and withered and fell away or were excommunicated.

John Bennett was not satisfied with the confusion that he and his conspirators caused, including the death of the Prophet. To justify his nefarious deeds, and his fall from authority in the Church, he then published a book under the title, *The History of the Saints; or an Expose of Joe Smith and Mormonism,* which reflected the hypocrisy and corrupt nature of the man. He claimed that he only joined the Church so that he could learn its secrets and expose its deception to the world.

After the Church was established in the west, the practice of **plural marriage** was publicly proclaimed. Interestingly it was Orson Pratt whom Brigham Young asked to present on July 24, 1859, the doctrine and practice of **polygamy** to the Church. From that day forward condemnation increased, promoted by the press and writers of various persuasions.

Pressure mounted in Congress to bring these Mormons to heel. One of Brigham's wives, Eliza, had filed for a divorce, and then embarked on a highly publicized national lecture tour denouncing **polygamy.** She finally appeared in Congress in April 1873 with an impassioned plea for the abolishment of **polygamy.**

Federal troops under Colonel Albert Johnston were sent at great expense in 1857 to stem the "rebellion" in Utah, followed by the California volunteers under Colonel Patrick Conner in 1862. The several U.S. Presidents sent territorial governors, judges and petty officials to administer authority and justice to the Mormon polygamists, not recognizing that the great majority of the Saints were not engaged in **polygamy.**

Congress passed legislation intended to suppress **polygamy,** the last of which was the Edmunds-Tucker Act in 1887. Elder Francis Gibbons has stated:

> This act contained stringent new provisions to penalize the Church and those practicing **polygamy.** The message said the Church was passing through a period of "transition and evolution" such as appeared "to be necessary in the progress and perfecting of all created things." It concluded with this

optimistic forecast: "The result will be that we shall be stronger, wiser, purer, happier, for the experience gained, and the work of the Lord . . . will yet triumph gloriously over all its foes" (Francis M. Gibbons, *Dynamic Disciples*, 81).

While federal efforts to suppress the practice of **plural marriage** was highly troublesome to the Saints, the open declaration of its practice created confusion and resistance for the missionaries, who tried to explain the doctrine and practice to monogamous-minded investigators.

> The effect of this proclamation [pronounced by Orson Pratt] gave opponents of the work great advantage, for in every foreign mission came reports of increased opposition resulting in many cases of mob violence—islands of the sea, from Denmark, Sweden and Norway; from distant India as well as from England and the United States. . . . The great number that were excommunicated from the church in 1852–1853 is generally referred to as indicating the effect of the official proclamation of this doctrine to the world . . . in the British Islands—show that the enormous number of seventeen hundred and seventy-six persons were excommunicated there during the first six months of the preaching of **polygamy**. The entire church then numbered, men, women, and children over eight years of age, 30,690. . . . That all these persons withdrew from the fellowship of the Mormon church on account of **polygamy** would be an unfair inference. Still, doubtless **polygamy** was the great cause of apostasy (B. H. Roberts, *Comprehensive History of the Church*, 4:59).

Federal persecution and prosecution intensified until the survival of the Church seemed in peril. All Church assets were seized; it was imminent that temples would be violated by Federal officers; and virtually all of the Church leaders were in hiding, paralyzing the administration of Church programs.

President Wilford Woodruff and his associates petitioned the Lord repeatedly for direction in this crisis. There was sufficient resolve to continue on practicing **plural marriage,** if the Lord commanded. Finally, President Woodruff received a revelation from the Lord that the practice of **polygamy** was to cease, bringing great relief to all of the Saints, and to the Congress and its agencies. The official declaration was issued October 6, 1890, and known as the Manifesto, which withdrew from the Saints the privilege of "contracting any marriage forbidden by the law of the land" (D&C OD–1).

This action began a process of healing. It ended the underground for men like Joseph F. Smith who now could live normally. Polygamists were granted amnesty for **plural marriages** solemnized before the Manifesto. Church properties escheated to the government were returned to the Church. And judges and prosecutors administered the laws benignly so as not to disrupt relationships created before the Manifesto. While a small group of Saints rejected the revelation, the great majority accepted it, recognizing that the prophetic authority that began **plural marriage** could end it and that ending it did not imply it was morally or theologically wrong.

The fight over **polygamy** ruined the Church financially. For several years after the Manifesto, the Church operated on borrowed money. This condition existed when Lorenzo Snow became President of the Church in September 1898. At the April 1899 general conference, several of the brethren talked about tithing. In his remarks on the subject, President [Joseph F.] Smith said in part, "I believe the Lord designs in this principle to test the obedience of the people." The Saints soon were put to that test in a remarkable way. The following month President Snow spoke to the Saints in St. George about the Lord blessing them in their distress if they would pay faithfully their tithing. Tithing doubled during the first year, and within a few years, the Church was debt free and the members enjoyed increased prosperity (Francis M. Gibbons, *Dynamic Disciples*, 143–45).

Years later, Brigham H. Roberts would declare:

> Those who refer to "Mormon **polygamy**" as a menace to the American home, or as a serious factor in American problems, make themselves ridiculous. So far as **plural marriage** is concerned, the question is settled. The problem of polygamous living among our people is rapidly solving itself. It is a matter of record that in 1890, when the Manifesto was issued, there were 2,451 plural families; in nine years this number had been reduced to 1,543. Four years later the number was 897; and many of these have since passed away (B. H. Roberts, *Comprehensive History of the Church*, 6:436).

While the overall atmosphere regarding **polygamy** gradually improved, the lives of the participants were not always tranquil. Brigham Young's son, John W., was the husband of five wives, four of whom left him. One of them wrote, "My children will never know in this life what the word father means," evidently referring to the absence of John in pursuit of extensive business ventures and the inability to spend time with five separate families. In 1903 John was sorely tried when one of his sons was convicted in a bizarre New York murder case and sentenced for life in Sing Sing prison (Dean C. Jesse, *Letters of Brigham Young to His Sons*, 88).

Many wives endured the loneliness and the need to provide for themselves and their children. Annie Tanner, one of six wives of John Tanner, tells of her years of moving from town to town, to live for interim periods of time with sympathetic members to protect her husband from prosecution and jail. Then when she had born ten children, six of whom were at home, John came to her one Sunday to say that he would not come there again. Furthermore, it was implied that she would not receive any further financial support.

Many Mormon couples, who were invited to participate in **plural marriage,** declined. Often they left the Church, returning to their former homes in the Midwest, or they moved on to California.

The majority of the Saints, who were not participants in **plural marriages,** were sympathetic to those who had responded to the call. But they all were to suffer from Federal prosecution and the interference of adventurers and riffraff who were drawn to expose or profit from the situation. It was another test for the Saints, unlike but just as wearing on them as it had been their trials in Missouri and Nauvoo.

The legacy of **polygamy** has persisted to our day in the minds of many uninformed, or uncaring, people throughout the world. On the other hand, so many descendants of polygamous families have mixed feelings about their heritage. Most feel some pride in their polygamous forefathers, and speak in awe of the challenge it was for their grandparents. Some do not regard well their polygamous forefathers. And a still smaller number have endeavored to live in **polygamy** to our day, outside of the sanctions and brotherhood of the Church.

For the faithful, the Manifesto clearly brought to close the practice of **plural marriage** in the Church of Jesus Christ of Latter-day Saints.

ENDURING TO THE END

The story is told of a conversation between U.S. Ambassador Andrew White and Count Leo Tolstoi, the great Russian author, statesman, and philosopher. Count Tolstoi asked Dr. White to tell him about your American religion. When Dr. White failed to identify such a religion, Count Tolstoi asked:

"What can you tell me of the teaching of the Mormons?"

"Well," said Dr. White, "I know very little concerning them. They have an unsavory reputation, they practice polygamy, and are very superstitious."

Then Count Leo Tolstoi, in his honest and stern, but lovable manner, rebuked the ambassador. "Dr. White, I am greatly surprised and disappointed that a man of your great learning and position should be so ignorant on this important subject. The Mormon people teach the American religion; their principles teach the people not only of heaven and its attendant glories, but how to live so that their social and economic relations with each other are placed on a sound basis. If the people follow the teachings of this Church, nothing can stop their progress—it will be limitless. There have been great movements started in the past, but they have died or been modified before they reached maturity. If Mormonism is able to **endure**, unmodified, until it reaches the third and fourth generations, it is destined to become the greatest power the world has ever known" (Alvin R. Dyer, *The Meaning of Truth*, 123).

While we have considered several of the major causes of apostasy, there are many others that can, and may, vary with the individual member. This was evident with those who braved the persecutions of Kirtland, Missouri and Nauvoo, wherein some kept the faith and others fell away or joined the persecutors. And it is particularly true for us today, in times when conditions are more complex and subtle.

As we embark on the twenty-first century, apostasy from the Church of Jesus Christ remains a great tragedy and a huge challenge, not only for Church leaders but for each of us under the injunction of the second great commandment—to love our neighbors as ourselves.

The magnitude of apostasy in the Church is not available, either in the early days or today. Average attendance of members of record is reportedly about 50 percent. But does this figure include what must be thousands of members whose whereabouts are not known, most of whom do not want to be found by the Church?

Then, how would one regard those in our wards and branches who do not attend, do not contribute tithes and offerings, will not accept calls to serve, and neglect or refuse to participate with the Saints? Are they in apostasy? Is their inactivity due to the causes cited in previous chapters?

Wilford Woodruff commented in 1880 that "there is hardly a tithe of the people who have been baptized in water for the remission of sins that have died in the faith. In the United States there are tens of thousands of apostate Mormons" (Wilford Woodruff, *Journal of Discourses* [1880], 21:281).

Governor Thomas Ford reported in his *History of Illinois* that only about 1,000 Mormons did not join the exodus from Nauvoo. However, there were groups of Saints at St. Louis, in Illinois and Iowa, cities in the East, and overseas, where many never gathered to Utah, in part because they could not afford it. Many more departed from the faith after polygamy was officially proclaimed in 1859.

138

Fortunate are the families who do not have parents, children or relatives who have chosen to absent themselves from communion with the faithful. Unfortunately, those who repent and return to the fold are far fewer that those who are leaving.

Brigham Young gave this encouragement regarding those who had apostatized:

> And the children and grand-children of those who apostatized years and years ago, will come up to Zion by hundreds and thousands, impelled by what their parents taught them in childhood (Brigham Young, *Journal of Discourses*, 14:195). [1871]

Elder David B. Haight has declared, "There are tens of thousands of good people who have quietly drifted away and are now waiting for a knock on their door. Those who have strayed must experience a doctrinal conversion and social integration by someone who cares" (David B. Haight, *A Light unto the World*, 114).

Elder John Morgan told the Saints in 1881:

> In our travels in the South we often meet with families who were once members of the Church, who during the trying times of Missouri and Illinois, or at some other time in the history of the Church, had stopped by the way- side—and where they stopped temporally they stopped spiritually; the cessation of their temporal work was the milestone that marked their spiritual resting place—but notwithstanding this falling away on the part of their parents, we found, as a general thing, that in the hearts of their children there was a love for the principles of eternal truth; and that if an elder was known to be in their vicinity they would send for him and make themselves known to him, and ninety-nine times out of a hundred they would ask to be baptized (John Morgan, *Journal of Discourses*, 23:39). [1881]

Authors Otten and Caldwell remind us:

Sometimes a member of the Church has difficulty staying active and faithful in the Church. Such
difficulty sometimes arises from acts of hypocrisy and
the resulting negative influence seen in the lives of
some members of the Church. When such an individual allows hypocrisy in the lives of others to justify his
own failure to perform according to his covenants, he
is doing so because he has not come to an understanding of the Lord's counsel. He has been deceived.
As early as 1831, the Lord revealed that there were
deceivers and hypocrites in the Church and warned of
the possible destructive influence such people might
have in the lives of the members (See D&C 50:4–7) The
Lord said that . . . He will deal with the hypocrite in
this life or in the next. . . . No one needs to be deceived
by the hypocritical actions of some who have membership standing in the Church whose motives are not
pure when they fail to live by the standards of the
Church (L. G. Otten and C. M. Caldwell, *Sacred Truths
of the Doctrine and Covenants*, 243).

President Young gave a stern warning to us:

One of the first steps to apostasy is to find fault
with your Bishop; and when that is done, unless
repented of a second step is soon taken, and by and by
the person is cut off from the Church, and that is the
end of it. Will you allow yourselves to find fault with
your Bishop? No; but come to me, go to the High
Council, or to the President of the Stake, and ascertain
whether your Bishop is doing wrong, before you find
fault and suffer yourselves to speak against a presiding officer (Brigham Young, *Journal of Discourses*,
9:141). [1861]

Brigham Young declared to the saints:

You may hear many say, "I am a Latter-day Saint,
and I never will apostatize; I am a Latter-day Saint, and
shall be to the day of my death." I never make such
declarations, and never shall. I think I have learned
that of myself I have no power, but my system is orga-

nized to increase in wisdom, knowledge, and power, and my wisdom is foolishness; then I cling to the Lord, and I have power in his name. I think I have learned the Gospel so as to know, that in and of myself I am nothing (John A. Widstoe, *Discourses of Brigham Young*, 1:337, 84).

His counselor, George Q. Cannon, gave further counsel:

We live in a day when we cannot trifle with God. He has said that His Spirit shall not always strive with man; He will withdraw that Spirit from us if we do not follow out His commands, and we shall be left to ourselves. The most dreadful condition that I can imagine a human being to be in is this, for a man who has once tasted of the word of God, who has felt its power, who has had a foretaste of the powers of the world to come, and who has rejoiced in those blessings, to suffer the spirit of God to depart from him through his own acts.

Whenever I have thought of it concerning myself, I have been filled with inexpressible horror. It has seemed as though a thousand deaths would be preferable, for to die is an easy thing; it is a light matter compared with apostasy, the loss of the Spirit of God, the forfeiting of the favor of heaven, the loss of interest in the work of God, to have the Spirit fade and withdrew itself from us until we live without it. Can you imagine any worse condition? (George Q. Cannon, *Gospel Truth*, 486).

The responsibility for each of us is clearly charged in three scriptures that are identified with the great welfare program of the Church:

And also, ye yourselves will succor those that stand in need of your succor; ye will administer of your substance unto him that standeth in need; and ye will not suffer that the beggar putteth up his petition to you in vain, and turn him out to perish (Mosiah 4:16).

> My beloved brethren, I say unto you, do not suppose
> that this is all; for after ye have done all these things,
> if ye turn away the needy, and the naked, and visit not
> the sick and afflicted, and impart of your substance, if
> ye have, to those who stand in need—I say unto you,
> if ye do not any of these things, behold, your prayer is
> vain, and availeth you nothing, and ye are as hyp-
> ocrites who do deny the faith (Alma 34:28).

> Therefore, if any man shall take of the abun-
> dance which I have made, and impart not his portion,
> according to the law of my gospel, unto the poor and
> the needy, he shall, with the wicked, lift up his eyes in
> hell, being in torment (D&C 104:18).

Ofttimes it is perceived that the Lord in these three
scriptures is counseling us to give of our temporal substance only. Upon closer examination, we can see that we
are to administer to the needs and wants of others, who
may be in great need of things that are less tangible. Such
needs might include sympathy, a listening ear, fixing an
appliance, moving household goods, a priesthood blessing,
advice, a compliment, comfort, and a thousand similar
kindnesses that will help another through a problem or a
lonely time. But there is the clear charge for us to seek
out those in need, not waiting for the Bishop to call us
forth, although we are under the obligation always to assist
the Bishop and his associates in their great duty to care
for the Saints.

George Q. Cannon gave a positive view of apostasy
and its effect on the Church:

> And yet I am thankful that people cannot stay in
> this Church and practice unrighteousness. I am thank-
> ful that God allows those who could not keep his com-
> mandments to fall away, so that his Church may be
> **cleansed.** . . . No man can stand in this Church, or
> retain the Spirit of God and continue in a course of
> hypocrisy for any length of time.

God will tear away the covering of lies and expose the wrong; he will leave the transgressor to himself, and the strength that he formerly had, which enabled him to stand and maintain his associations with the people of God, will be taken away from him, and he will go down to destruction unless he repents (George Q. Cannon, *Journal of Discourses* [1875], 18:84).

We have been mobbed, tried and persecuted in various ways, but all these things have had the effect of **cleansing** us, they have all had their purpose. I would not give much for this Church today if all who had joined it were members of it—this is, members of it with their sins and corruptions and inclinations to do wrong. I am thankful for one thing connected with this work, namely, that every trial has the effect of **cleansing** the Church, of keeping it pure, of taking away from it the dross and leaving the somewhat purer element. . . . This Church . . . has the power of self-purification (George Q. Cannon, *Journal of Discourses*, 22:243). [1881]

Elder Jeffrey R. Holland observed that **enduring** is as essential to Nephi's "doctrine of Christ," as are faith, repentance, baptism and bestowal of the Holy Ghost:

Often one hears trite, sometimes consciously apologetic references to "**enduring to the end**" as an addition to the first principles and ordinances of the gospel. Nevertheless, the doctrine of faithful **endurance** is infinitely serious, and it is here declared to be a basic principle of the gospel by the God and Father of us all. "**Enduring to the end**" is an integral element in the doctrine of Christ (Jeffrey R. Holland, *Christ and the New Covenant*, 54).

Apostle Neal A. Maxwell suggests some dimensions of **enduring**:

To think of **enduring to the end** as "hanging in there," doing one's duty relentlessly, is not inaccurate.

Yet **enduring to the end** is more than outlasting and surviving, though it includes those qualities. We are called upon, as was the Prophet Joseph, to "**endure** it well," gracefully, not grudgingly. (D&C 121:8). We are also told that we must "**endure** in faith" (D&C 101:35). These dimensions of **enduring** are important to note. Likewise, we are asked to **endure** "valiantly," (D&C 121:29). . . . **Enduring** the sense of our inadequacy in the face of callings is more common than we know. We are also asked to **endure** temptation (James 1:12). The growing coarseness of our times suggests that, like Lot in Sodom, we may be "vexed with the filthy conversation of the wicked" (2 Peter 2:7)—just one more way in which we must **endure** evil in our environments (Neal A. Maxwell, *Wherefore, Ye must Press Forward*, 109).

But if we share Elder Maxwell's view that our environment is deteriorating, the prophecies suggest that it will become worse as we near the Second Coming of Jesus Christ.

As conditions deteriorate, the faith of the Saints will be tried. Elder Heber C. Kimball, a man of great prophetic gifts, warned the Saints:

The time will come when no man nor woman will be able to **endure** on borrowed light. Each will have to be guided by the light within himself . . . . .You will have all the persecution you want and more too, and all the opportunity to show your integrity to God and truth that you could desire (Orson F. Whitney, *The Life of Heber C. Kimball*, 450).

Brigham Young warned the Saints:

If the Saints neglect to **pray**, and violate the day that is set apart for the worship of God, they will lose his **Spirit**. If a man shall suffer himself to be overcome with anger, and curse and swear, taking the name of the Deity in vain, he cannot retain the **Holy Spirit**. In short, if a man shall do anything which he knows to be wrong, and repenteth not, he cannot enjoy the

Holy Spirit, but will walk in darkness and ultimately deny the faith (Brigham Young, _Journal of Discourses_ [1865], 11:134).

Many receive the Gospel because they know it is true; they are convinced in their judgment that it is true. . . . They yield to it, and obey its first principles, but never seek to be enlightened by the power of the **Holy Ghost**, such ones frequently step out of the way (Brigham Young, _Journal of Discourses_, 2:250). [1855]

At an earlier time, Jesus warned the Twelve in Galilee: "And ye shall be hated of all men for my name's sake, but he that **endureth to the end** shall be saved" (Matt. 10:22).

To the multitude in the land Bountiful, the resurrected Jesus appeared and taught them:

I am the law, and the light. Look unto me, and **endure to the end**, and ye shall live; for unto him that **endureth to the end** will I give eternal life (3 Ne.15:9).

Elder Bruce R. McConkie observed that in these last days conditions would become increasingly perilous and confounding:

In the very nature of things, the signs of the times will not cease until the Lord comes. Those that involve chaos and commotion and distress of nations will continue in the future with even greater destructive force. Men's hearts will fail them for fear in greater degree hereafter than heretofore. Wars will get worse. Moments of armistice and peace will be less stable. Viewed in the perspective of years, all worldly things will degenerate. There will be an increasing polarization of views. There will be more apostasy from the Church, more summer saints and sunshine patriots who will be won over to the cause of the adversary. . . . While the faithful Saints get better and better, and cleave more firmly to the heaven-sent standards, the world will get worse and worse and will cleave to the policies and views of Lucifer.

Among the specific signs that lie ahead are the building of the New Jerusalem and the rebuilding of the Jerusalem of old. The great conference at Adam-ondi-Ahman must yet be held. The two prophets must minister and be martyred in Jerusalem. The gloom and despair and death of Armageddon must yet cover the earth; Babylon must fall; the vineyard must be burned; and then the earth shall rest and the Lord Jesus shall rule and reign for the space of a thousand years. But before that great day there shall be signs and wonders of a marvelous kind shown forth in heaven and on earth (Bruce R. McConkie, *The Millennial Messiah*, 405).

So it is with us, if we choose to rely on our own wisdom to survive the myriad temptations that are daily bombarding us. Satan has unleashed a Pandora's Box of worldly, evil influences that invite us to "eat, drink and be merry," without restraint.

But God, who loves us, has warned and promised us that we can prevail, if we are vigilant and obedient. His apostle Paul, wrote to his "beloved son," Timothy, concerning our day that ominous conditions will sorely test the faithfulness and **endurance** of the Saints.

In the last days perilous times shall come.

For men shall be lovers of their ownselves, covetous, boasters, proud, blasphemers, disobedient to parents, unthankful, unholy,

Without natural affection, trucebreakers, false accusers, incontinent, fierce, despisers of those that are good,

Traitors, heady, highminded, lovers of pleasures more than lovers of God;

Having a form of godliness, but denying the power thereof: . . .

Ever learning, and never able to come to the knowledge of the truth. . . .

> For the time will come when they will not
> **endure** sound doctrine; but after their own lusts shall
> they heap to themselves teachers, having itching ears;
>
> And they shall turn away their ears from the truth,
> and shall be turned unto fables (2 Tim. 3:1–5, 7; 4:3–4).

In a vision Nephi also saw and described the latter days in the bringing forth of the gospel to the Gentiles and the remnant of Lehi in the promised land. He declared:

> And blessed are they who shall seek to bring forth my
> Zion at that day, for they shall have the gift and the
> power of the **Holy Ghost**; and if they **endure unto
> the end** they shall be lifted up at the last day, and shall
> be saved in the everlasting kingdom of the Lamb
> (1 Ne. 13:37).

Recall the dream of Brigham Young when the Prophet Joseph Smith came to him with this advice: "Tell the brethren if they follow the spirit of the Lord they will go right. Be sure to **tell the people to keep the Spirit.**"

President Marion G. Romney told the students at Brigham Young University: "If you want to obtain and keep the guidance of the Spirit, you can do so by following this simple four-point program:

> One, **pray**. Pray diligently. . . . Learn to talk to the
> Lord; call upon his name in great faith and confidence.
>
> Second, **study** and learn the gospel.
>
> Third, **live righteously; repent** of your sins by
> confessing them and forsaking them. Then **conform** to
> the teachings of the gospel.
>
> Fourth, give **service** in the Church.

Regarding this last invitation to service, there are so many opportunities for each of us to continue to serve not only in the Church but in our personal activities. Home and visiting teaching can invigorate our lives as we faithfully administer to the needs of those to whom we are assigned.

There are so many opportunities for seniors to serve missions in a variety of places and capacities. With the proliferation of temples worldwide, there is a great demand for temple ordinance workers; and the blessings of this service are marvelous in retaining the Spirit.

Elder Alexander W. Morrison suggests that **service to others** is the hallmark of the life of the Lord's shepherd-leaders:

> It is the highest expression of Christian stewardship. **Service** to others drives out selfishness, the great enemy of spirituality. Subduing the ego permits soul growth and signifies the extent of our devotion to Christ and His cause. It is the mark of true greatness of character. Jesus knew that and exemplified it in His life. Said He, "Whosoever will be great among you, let him be your minister; and whosoever will be chief among you, let him be your servant" (Matthew 20:26–27) (Alexander W. Morrison, *Feed My Sheep*, 47).

Since pride seems to underlie virtually all of the causes of apostasy, we would be well advised to follow a course of thought and behavior that avoids prideful ways. We would be wise to **cultivate the traits of humility, meekness, modesty and submissiveness.** Our Church leaders exhibit these attributes, as do many others, notably the elderly. We need to become acquainted with these exemplars, either by personal contact if they live near us, or in studying the lives of those who are not directly available to us. Stories and biographies of our faithful forefathers, with an emphasis on their laudable traits, should be pursued. The profiles of the sixty faithful pioneers in the companion volume are examples of heroes worthy of our emulation.

The teaching and experiencing of the **Holy Spirit** in our personal lives and in our families is highly desirable. We should **cultivate personal habits and worthiness** that qualify us for the promptings of the **Spirit.** Our missionaries are taught to help their investigators to recognize the special feelings in their personal experiences as coming from the **Holy Ghost.** We need to do the same in our family nights and councils.

The **Holy Spirit** is God's messenger to each of us. If we are worthy to receive His promptings and enlightenment, we shall know how to walk the true path to the tree in Lehi's dream. Furthermore, we will have the wisdom to discern between truth and error, good and evil, and to make correct choices. We will not have an appetite for the lustful, base, and vulgar things of the world.

We also must determine that we will go where the **Holy Spirit** can be **found—temples, chapels, homes, and mountain tops—quiet places** where we can hear the still, small voice of the **Spirit.** We must see and hear from sources that abide spiritual things: the scriptures, Church manuals and magazines, classics, inspirational music and videos, nature and animals, physical exercise and work, creative hobbies, and service to others, especially those in need of our comfort and personal attention. These pursuits will bring the **Spirit** into our souls and refine our sensitivities to the sweet and gentle whisperings of the **Spirit.**

It is the **Spirit** that prepares us to become a Zion people, wherein we practice the second great commandment to love our neighbors as ourselves. This concept should be taught, learned and practiced in our families, so that we are able to practice it when we venture into the wicked world. It is there where we may realize the supernal joy of bringing the prodigal home or to gather into the fold of God those who are seeking the true gospel of Jesus Christ.

We need not wonder where to turn for guidance, if we follow the counsel given by the prophet Nephi:

> For behold, again I say unto to you that if ye will
> enter in by the way, and receive the Holy Ghost, it

will show unto you all things what ye should do
(2 Ne. 32:2–5).

In the words of Joseph Smith, we "believe all things, we
hope all things, we have **endured** many things, and hope
to be able to **endure** all things" (A of F 13).

In June 1829 the Lord gave this promise to the early
Saints before the Church was organized:

> And, if you keep my commandments and
> **endure to the end** you shall have eternal life, which
> gift is the greatest of all the gifts of God (D&C 14:7).

Thus we can rely on the promise of our Savior regarding the requirement for life with Him and our Eternal
Father in the eternities. We must **endure to the end.**

The Prophet Nephi provides some guidelines in his
great farewell sermon on the doctrine of Christ:

> And I heard a voice from the Father, saying: Yea,
> the words of my Beloved are true and faithful. He that
> **endureth to the end**, the same shall be saved.

> And now, my beloved brethren, I know by this
> that unless a man shall **endure to the end,** in follow-
> ing the example of the son of the living God, he can-
> not be saved.

> Wherefore, do the things which I have told you I
> have seen that your Lord and your Redeemer should
> do; for, for this cause have they been shown unto me,
> that ye might know the gate by which ye should enter.
> For the gate by which ye should enter is repentance
> and baptism by water; and then cometh a remission of
> your sins by fire and by the Holy Ghost.

> And then are ye in this strait and narrow path
> which leads to eternal life; yea, ye have entered in by
> the gate; ye have done according to the command-
> ments of the Father and the Son, unto the fulfilling of
> the promise which he hath made, that if ye entered in
> by the way ye shall receive.

Wherefore, ye must press forward with a stead-fastness in Christ, having a perfect brightness of hope, and a love of God and of all men. Wherefore, if ye shall press forward feasting upon the word of Christ, and **endure to the end,** behold, thus saith the Father, ye shall have eternal life.

And now, behold, my beloved brethren, this is the way; and there is none other way nor name given under heaven whereby man can be saved in the king-dom of God. And now, this is the doctrine of Christ, and the only and true doctrine of the Father, and of the Son, and of the Holy Ghost, which is one God, with-out end (2 Ne. 31:15–21).

Joseph Smith had **endured**, even to giving his mortal life. He was permitted to return to his successor to counsel us in how we can **endure to the end** of our lives.

Brigham Young lay ill in Winter Quarters, when the Prophet Joseph Smith came to him in a night vision or a dream on February 23, 1847. Brother Young said that Joseph told him:

Tell the people to be humble and faithful, and be sure to keep the **spirit of the Lord** and it will lead them right. Be careful and not turn away the small still voice; it will teach you what to do and where to go; it will yield the fruits of the kingdom. Tell the brethren to keep their hearts open to conviction, so that when the **Holy Ghost** comes to them, their hearts will be ready to receive it. They can tell the **Spirit of the Lord** from all other spirits; it will whisper peace and joy to their souls; it will take malice, hatred, strife and all evil from their hearts; and their whole desire will be to do good, bring forth righteousness and build up the kingdom of God. Tell the brethren if they will follow the **spirit of the Lord**, they will go right. Be sure to tell the people to keep the **spirit of the Lord**." Joseph said again, "Tell the people to be sure to keep the **Spirit of the Lord** and follow it, and it will lead them just right." (Brigham Young, *Manuscript History of Brigham Young*, from the *Millennial Star*)

We are assured by a prophet, Gordon B. Hinckley, in our day:

> I leave my blessing upon you. The Savior lives. This is His church. The work is true, and in the words of our Lord and Savior, "Look unto me, and **endure to the end**, and ye shall live; for unto him that **endureth to the end** will I give eternal life" (3rd Nephi 15:9), to which I testify in the name of Jesus Christ, amen (Gordon B. Hinckley, *Listen to a Prophet's Voice*, 82).

RESEARCH SOURCES FOR
ENDURING TO THE END

Arrington, Leonard, and Davis Bitton. *Saints without Halos.* Salt Lake City: Signature Books, 1981.

Asay, Carlos E. *Family Pecan Trees.* Salt Lake City: Deseret Book, 1992.

Ballard, M. Russell. *Counseling with Our Councils.* Salt Lake City: Deseret Book, 1997.

Barrett, Ivan J. *Joseph Smith and the Restoration.* Provo: Brigham Young University Press, 1968.

Benson, Ezra Taft. *So Shall We Reap.* Salt Lake City: Deseret Book, 1960.

Black, Susan Easton. *Who's Who in the Doctrine and Covenants.* Salt Lake City: Bookcraft, 1997.

The Book of Mormon. Salt Lake City: The Church of Jesus Christ of Latter-day Saints, 1981.

Brown, Hugh B. *Continuing the Quest.* Salt Lake City: Deseret Book, 1961.

Burton, Alma P. *Discourses of the Prophet Joseph Smith.* Salt Lake City, 1977.

Cannon, George Q. *Gospel Truths.* Salt Lake City: Deseret Book, 1987.

Cannon, George Q. *Life of Joseph Smith the Prophet.* Salt Lake City: Deseret Book, 1964.

Cook, Gene R. *Raising Up a Child Unto the Lord.* Salt Lake City: Deseret Book, 1993.

Cook, Lyndon W. *The Revelations of the Prophet Joseph Smith.* Salt Lake City: Deseret Book, 1981.

Cowley, Matthias F. *Wilford Woodruff, His Life and Labors.* Salt Lake City: Bookcraft, 1964.

Doctrine and Covenants. Salt Lake City: The Church of Jesus Christ of Latter-day Saints, 1981.

Dyer, Alvin R. *The Meaning of Truth.* Salt Lake City: Deseret Book, 1961.

Eyring, Henry B. *To Draw Closer to God.* Salt Lake City: Deseret Book, 1997.

Faust, James E. *Finding Light in a Dark World.* Salt Lake City: Deseret Book, 1995.

Flake, Lawrence. *Mighty Men of Zion.* Salt Lake City: K. D. Butler, 1974.

Gibbons, Francis M. *Dynamic Disciples, Prophets of the Lord.* Salt Lake City: Deseret Book, 1996.

Godfrey, Kenneth. *Women's Voices: An Untold History of the Latter-day Saints.* Salt Lake City: Deseret Book, 1982.

Gordon, Leo V., and Richard Vetterli. *Powderkeg: The Story of the Mormons.* Novata, Calif.: Presidio Press, 1991.

Hafen, Bruce C. *The Broken Heart.* Salt Lake City: Deseret Book, 1989.

Hafen, LeRoy R., and Ann W. Hafen, eds. *Handcarts to Zion: The Story of a Unique Western Migration, 1856–1860 ; with Contemporary Journals, Accounts, Reports, and Rosters of Members of the Ten Handcart Companies.* The Far West and the Rockies historical series, 1820–75, vol. 14. Glendale, Calif.: Arthur H. Clark, 1960.

Hinckley, Gordon B. *Teachings of Gordon B. Hinckley.* Salt Lake City: Deseret Book, 1997.

Holland, Jeffrey R. *Christ and the New Covenant.* Salt Lake City: Deseret Book, 1997.

The Holy Bible. Salt Lake City: Church of Jesus Christ of Latter-day Saints, 1979.

Hunter, Howard W. *That We Might Have Joy.* Salt Lake City: Deseret Book, 1994.

Hunter, Milton R. *Will a Man Rob God?* Salt Lake City: Deseret Book, 1952.

Jensen, Andrew. *Latter-day Saint Biographical Encyclopedia: A Compilation of Biographical Sketches of Prominent Men and Women in The Church of Jesus Christ of Latter-day Saints.* 4 vols. Salt Lake City: Andrew Jenson History, 1901–36. Reprint. Salt Lake City: Western Epics, 1971.

Jesse, Dean C. *Letters of Brigham Young to His Sons.* Salt Lake City: Deseret Book, 1974.

Journal of Discourses. 26 vols. Liverpool: F. D. Richards, 1855–86.

Kimball, Edward L. *Teachings of Spencer W. Kimball.* Salt Lake City: Bookcraft, 1982.

Kimball, Spencer W. *Faith Precedes the Miracle.* Salt Lake City: Deseret Book, 1972.

Kimball, Spencer W. *The Miracle of Forgiveness.* Salt Lake City: Bookcraft, 1992.

Lee, Harold B. *Decisions for Successful Living.* Salt Lake City: Deseret Book, 1973.

Lee, Harold B. *Stand Ye in Holy Places.* Salt Lake City: Deseret Book, 1974.

Maxwell, Neal A. *Look Back at Sodom.* Salt Lake City: Deseret Book, 1975.

Maxwell, Neal A. *Meek and Lowly.* Salt Lake City: Deseret Book, 1987.

Maxwell, Neal A. *Things as They Really Are.* Salt Lake City: Deseret Book, 1978.

McConkie, Bruce R. *Millennial Messiah.* Salt Lake City: Deseret Book, 1982.

McConkie, Bruce R. *Mormon Doctrine.* Salt Lake City: Bookcraft, 1966.

McCracken, Robert J. *What Is Sin? What Is Virtue?* New York: Harper & Rowe, 1966.

155

McCune, George M. *Personalities in the Doctrine and Covenants and Joseph Smith-History.* Salt Lake City: Hawkes Publishing, 1991.

Morrison, Alexander B. *Feed My Sheep.* Salt Lake City: Deseret Book, 1992.

Morrison, Alexander B. *Visions of Zion.* Salt Lake City: Deseret Book, 1993.

Nelson, Lee. *Wakara.* Mapleton, Utah: Council Press, 1990.

Otten, L. G., and C. M. Caldwell. *Sacred Truths of the Doctrine and Covenants.* 2 vols. Salt Lake City: Deseret Book, 1982.

The Pearl of Great Price. Salt Lake City: The Church of Jesus Christ of Latter-day Saints, 1981.

Pratt, Parley P. *The Autobiography of Parley P. Pratt.* Salt Lake City: Deseret Book, 1973.

Quinn, Michael. *The Mormon Hierarchy: Origins of Power.* Salt Lake City: Signature Books, 1994.

Reynolds, George, and Janne Sjodahl. *Commentary on the Book of Mormon.* Salt Lake City: Deseret Book, 1955.

Roberts, B. H. *A Comprehensive History of The Church of Jesus Christ of Latter-day Saints, Century One.* 6 vols. Salt Lake City: Deseret News Press, 1930. Salt Lake City: Corporation of the President, The Church of Jesus Christ of Latter-day Saints, 1965.

Roberts, Brigham H. *The Life of John Taylor.* Salt Lake City: Bookcraft, 1963.

Roberts, Brigham H. *New Witness for God.* Salt Lake City: George Q. Cannon & Sons, 1895.

Romney, Marion G. *Learning for the Eternities.* Salt Lake City: Deseret Book, 1977.

Smith, Hyrum M., and Janne M. Sjodahl. *Doctrine and Covenants Commentary.* Salt Lake City: Deseret Book, 1978.

Smith, Joseph, Jr. *History of the Church of Jesus Christ.* Salt Lake City: Deseret Book, 1950.

Smith, Joseph F. *Gospel Doctrine.* Salt Lake City: Deseret Book, 1919.

Smith, Joseph Fielding. *Answers to Gospel Questions.* Salt Lake City: Deseret Book, 1954.

Smith, Joseph Fielding. *Church History and Modern Revelation.* Salt Lake City: Deseret Book, 1947.

Smith, Joseph Fielding. *Take Heed to Yourselves.* Salt Lake City: Deseret Book, 1966.

Smith, Joseph Fielding, comp. *Teachings of the Prophet Joseph Smith.* Salt Lake City: Deseret Book, 1976.

Smith, Lucy Mack. *History of Joseph Smith.* Salt Lake City: Stevens and Wallis, 1945.

Talmage, James E. *Jesus the Christ.* Salt Lake City: Deseret Book, 1949.

Tullidge, Edward W. *Life of Joseph the Prophet.* New York: Tullidge & Crandall, 1878.

Van Noord, Roger. *King of Beaver Island.* Urbana: University of Illinois Press, 1988.

Van Wagoner, Richard, and Steven C. Walker. *A Book of Mormons.* Salt Lake City: Signature Books, 1982.

Walker, Ronald W. *Wayward Saints: The Godbeites and Brigham Young.* Urbana: University of Illinois Press, 1939.

Whitney, Orson F. *The Life of Heber C. Kimball.* 1888.

Widstoe, John A. *Discourses of Brigham Young.* Salt Lake City: Deseret Book, 1954.

Widstoe, John A. *Evidences and Reconciliations.* Salt Lake City: Bookcraft, 1972.

Widstoe, John A. *The Message of the Doctrine and Covenants.* Salt Lake City: Bookcraft, 1969.

Young, Brigham. *The Manuscript History of Brigham Young.* 1801–35. Printed in the *Millennial Star.*

Chronology of the Restoration

23 Dec 1805   Joseph Smith born at Sharon, Vermont.

Spring 1820   First vision—Father and Son appear to Joseph Smith (age 14).

21/22 Sep 1823 Moroni appears three times at night to Joseph Smith (age 17) at home and again in the nearby field the following day, after which he views the gold plates on the Hill Cumorah.

18 Jan 1827   Joseph Smith marries Emma Hale.

22 Sep 1827   Moroni delivers gold plates to Joseph Smith (age 21).

Feb 1828   Martin Harris takes the transcript of characters and their definitions to New York for verification.

Jun–Jul 1828   Martin Harris takes the 116 manuscript pages from Harmony and loses them at Palmyra, which caused Joseph to lose the gold plates and the ability to translate them.

7 Apr 1829   Joseph Smith resumes translation of the record with Oliver Cowdery as scribe.

15 May 1829   John the Baptist confers Aaronic Priesthood on Joseph Smith (age 23) and Oliver Cowdery (age 24); they baptize

each other in the Susquehanna River near Harmony, Pennsylvania.

May–Jun 1829 Peter, James and John confer the Melchizedek Priesthood upon Joseph Smith and Oliver Cowdery between Harmony and Colesville, New York.

Mar–Jun 1829 Joseph Smith translates the gold plates as the Book of Mormon.

June 1829 Three Witnesses are shown the gold plates by Moroni in Fayette, New York; 8 Witnesses are shown the gold plates by Joseph Smith in Manchester, New York.

26 Mar 1830 Book of Mormon is published.

6 Apr 1830 The "Church of Christ" is organized in Fayette, New York with 6 members.

9 Jun 1830 First conference of the Church held at Fayette.

1 Feb 1831 Joseph Smith arrives in Kirtland and commences ministry there.

4 Feb 1831 Edward Partridge ordained as the first Bishop.

3 Jun 1831 Joseph Smith is ordained to the High Priesthood (age 25).

6 Jun 1831 Sidney Rigdon designated as "spokesman" for Joseph Smith.

13 Oct 1831 Ezra Booth attacks the Church in *Ohio Star* newspaper.

25 Jan 1832 Joseph Smith (age 26) ordained as President of the High Priesthood by Sidney Rigdon.

16 Feb 1832 Joseph Smith and Sidney Rigdon see in vision the 3 Degrees of Glory (D&C 76).

8 Mar 1832	Jesse Gause (age 46) and Sidney Rigdon (age 39) are ordained as Counselors to Joseph Smith.
24 Mar 1832	Joseph Smith and Sidney Rigdon are tarred and feathered at Hiram, Ohio.
5 Jul 1832	Sidney Rigdon tries to seize control of the Church and is disfellowshipped.
3 Dec 1832	Jesse Gause is excommunicated.
27 Feb 1833	Revelation known as the Word of Wisdom is received by Joseph Smith (D&C 89).
25 Jun 1833	Joseph Smith describes to 24 brethren the Temple to be built at Independence.
2 Jul 1833	Joseph Smith (age 27) concludes the first translation of the Bible.
7 Nov 1833	Saints driven from Jackson County across the Missouri River.
18 Dec 1833	Joseph Smith Sr. is ordained as the first Church Patriarch.
17 Feb 1834	The first stake high council is organized at Kirtland, Ohio.
19 Apr 1834	Joseph Smith designates Sidney Rigdon to preside over the Church in his absence.
8 May 1834	Zion's Camp departs for Missouri.
7–8 Jul 1834	Joseph Smith ordains David Whitmer as successor if he doesn't live to God.
5 Dec 1834	Joseph Smith ordains Oliver Cowdery as Assistant President, ahead of his two Counselors.
14 Feb 1835	Quorum of the Twelve, chosen by the Three Witnesses, is organized at Kirtland.
28 Feb 1835	Council of Seventy organized with seven Presidents at Kirtland.

28 Mar 1835	Revelation received that First Presidency, Quorum of the Twelve and the First Quorum of the Seventy are equal in authority (D&C 107).
Jul 1835	Joseph Smith purchases the Egyptian mummies and papyrus .
14 Sep 1835	Emma Smith is appointed to select hymns for the Church (D&C 25).
3 Mar 1836	Elijah Abel (Negro) ordained an elder; on the following December 20, he is ordained a Seventy.
27 Mar 1836	Kirtland Temple is dedicated with great spiritual manifestations.
3 Apr 1836	Joseph Smith and Oliver Cowdery see Jesus Christ, Moses, Elias, and Elijah. and receive from them priesthood keys (D&C 110).
2 Nov 1836	Kirtland Safety Banking Society is organized.
13 Jun 1837	Apostles Brigham Young, Heber C. Kimball and Orson Hyde leave on the first mission to Europe.
22 Dec 1837	Apostates led by Warren Parrish seize the Kirtland Temple.
1 Jan 1838	Dozens of dissenters in Kirtland are excommunicated by the High Council, including Martin Harris.
14 Mar 1838	Headquarters of the Church established at Far West, Missouri.
13 Apr 1838	Excommunication of Oliver Cowdery, David Whitmer and Lyman Johnson at Far West, Missouri.

26 Apr 1838	Church name is changed to The Church of Jesus Christ of Latter-day Saints (D&C 115).
17 Jun 1838	Sidney Rigdon preaches "Salt Sermon" at Far West as a warning against dissenters.
4 Jul 1838	Sidney Rigdon preaches Independence Day sermon at Far West warning mobocrats of retribution by the Saints.
25 Oct 1838	Apostle David Patten killed at Crooked River skirmish.
27 Oct 1838	Governor Lilburn Boggs of Missouri issues "Exterminating Order."
30 Oct 1838	Missouri militia massacres 17 Mormon men and boys at Haun's Mill, Missouri.
31 Oct 1838	Joseph Smith and 40 brethren surrendered to Missouri militia by Colonel George Hinkle.
30 Nov 1838	Joseph Smith (age 32) and others are incarcerated at Liberty, Missouri, jail.
26 Jan 1839	Assistant Counselor John Smith and Apostle Brigham Young organize the exodus of the Saints from Missouri to Quincy, Illinois.
16 Apr 1839	Joseph Smith and other prisoners are allowed to escape from custody.
26 Apr 1839	The Twelve meet secretly at Far West and ordain Wilford Woodruff and George A. Smith as apostles.
29 Nov 1839	Joseph Smith (age 33) meets President Martin Van Buren, who tells him that the Federal Government can do nothing to help the Saints.

6 Jun 1840	First British converts reach Nauvoo.
15 Aug 1840	First baptisms for the dead are performed.
5 Apr 1841	Joseph Smith marries Louisa Beman as plural wife.
24 Oct 1841	At Jerusalem Orson Hyde dedicates Palestine for the restoration of the Jews.
1 Mar 1842	First Vision published; Wentworth Letter, containing the Articles of Faith, published.
15 Mar 1842	Joseph Smith becomes a Free Mason.
17 Mar 1842	Joseph Smith organizes the Female Relief Society at Nauvoo with Emma Smith as President.
7 Apr 1842	Revelation regarding the Council of Fifty received.
4 May 1842	First endowment ordinance given in the Red Brick Store, Nauvoo.
23 May 1843	Emma Smith approves two plural wives for Joseph Smith.
28 May 1843	Joseph and Emma Smith are sealed for eternity.
12 July 1843	Revelation regarding plural marriage and Celestial marriage given by Joseph Smith (D&C 132).
22 Aug 1843	Ward teaching introduced in Nauvoo.
28 Sep 1843	Joseph and Emma Smith receive Second Anointing, in which each is "anointed and ordained to the highest and holiest order of the priesthood."
11 Mar 1844	Council of Fifty is organized.
Apr–May 1844	Joseph Smith says that his unborn son David will be Church President.

7 Jun 1844	First and only edition of the apostate *Nauvoo Expositor* is published with libelous articles regarding the Prophet and the Church.
20 Jun 1844	Joseph Smith writes to the Twelve that they should return to Nauvoo immediately.
27 Jun 1844	Joseph (age 38) and Hyrum Smith (age 44) are martyred at Carthage, Illinois, Jail.
4 Aug 1844	Sidney Rigdon at Nauvoo offers to be Guardian of the Church.
5 Aug 1844	James J. Strang declares that Joseph Smith chose him to be his successor.
8 Aug 1844	Brigham Young is transfigured as Joseph Smith before a conference of the Saints.
24 May 1845	The Twelve ordain Apostle William Smith as Church Patriarch.
24 Sep 1845	Brigham Young signs an agreement that the Saints will leave Nauvoo.
1 Jan 1846	First sealing of a man and wife for time and eternity in Nauvoo Temple.
4 Feb 1846	First members depart Nauvoo across the Mississippi River; Saints under Sam Brannon depart New York harbor for California on the ship *Brooklyn*.
30 Jun 1846	U.S. Army requests 2,000 volunteers to march as soldiers to California; 500 volunteers are recruited as the Mormon Battalion.
17 Sep 1846	Mobs drive remaining Saints from Nauvoo following the Battle of Nauvoo.

14 Jan 1847	Brigham Young gives D&C 136 as organization for the pioneer march to the Rocky Mountains.
6 Apr 1847	Newel K. Whitney is appointed Presiding Bishop of the Church, without counselors.
21 Jul 1847	Orson Pratt and Erastus Snow enter Salt Lake valley.
24 Jul 1847	Vanguard company of pioneers enters Salt Lake valley.
23 Dec 1847	Emma Smith marries Major Lewis Bidamon on Joseph Smith's birthday.
27 Dec 1847	Brigham Young, Heber C. Kimball, and Willard Richards are sustained and ordained as the First Presidency at Kanesville, Iowa Territory.

CEDAR FORT, INCORPORATED
Order Form

Name:_____

Address: _____

City: _____ State: _____ Zip: _____

Phone: (   ) _____ Daytime phone: (   ) _____

Enduring to the End

Quantity: _____ @ $12.95 each: _____

plus $3.49 shipping & handling for the first book: _____

(add 99¢ shipping for each additional book)

Utah residents add 6.25% for state sales tax: _____

TOTAL: _____

Bulk purchasing, shipping and handling quotes available upon request.

Please make check or money order payable to:

Cedar Fort, Incorporated.

Mail this form and payment to:

Cedar Fort, Inc.

925 North Main St.

Springville, UT 84663

You can also order on our website **www.cedarfort.com**

or e-mail us at sales@cedarfort.com or call 1-800-SKYBOOK